the Pueblos

Bertha P. Dutton is a distinguished anthropologist and expert on the archaeology and ethnology of Southwestern and Meso-American Indians. Among her many publications are *Sun Father's Way, The Pueblo Indian World* (with E. L. Hewett), *Happy People: The Huichol Indians,* and numerous journal articles and reviews.

Her work in the field has included research projects and excavations throughout the Southwest and expeditions to Peru, Bolivia, Ecuador, Panama, Guatemala, and Mexico, as well as attendance at conferences in South America, Europe, and the Orient.

The New Mexico Press Women presented to Dr. Dutton in 1971 the coveted Zía award for outstanding publications, and in 1974 she was appointed New Mexico representative to the National Park Service's Southwest Regional advisory committee by Secretary of the Interior Rogers C. B. Morton. She is a Research Associate of the Museum of New Mexico in Santa Fe; for a decade she served as Director of the Museum of Navaho Ceremonial Art, Inc., in that city.

UTAH
NEV.
ARIZONA
CALIFORNIA
MEXI
SONORA
NAVAHO
HOPI
SHIVWITS
KAIBAB
HUALAPAI
MOHAVE
CHEMEHUEVI
COLORADO R.
FORT APACHE
SAN CARLOS
FT. McDOWELL
SALT R.
GILA BEND
GILA R.
MARICOPA
YUMA
COCOPAH
PAPAGO
SAN XAVIER
Cedar City
Monticello
Kanab
L. Powell
Virgin R.
L. Mead
Las Vegas
Colorado R.
Grand Canyon National Park
Tuba City
Many Farms
Chin
Window R
Flagstaff
Holbrook
Little Colorado R.
Big Sandy R.
Prescott
Parker
Springerville
Phoenix
Salt R.
Gila R.
Yuma
San Luis
Tucson
Sells
Nogales
Nogales
Doug
Gulf of California
0 50 75 100 miles
15
93
15
89
160
264
180
93
66
40
40
40
93
17
60
60
10
95
60
70
8
8
10
666
10
666
19

MAJOR INDIAN RESERVATIONS OF THE SOUTHWEST

This book and its two companion volumes,
Navahos and Apaches: The Athabascan Peoples and
The Rancheria, Ute, and Southern Paiute Peoples,
were originally published in one hardcover edition as
Indians of the American Southwest (Prentice-Hall, 1975).

the Pueblos

Bertha P. Dutton

PRENTICE-HALL, INC.   ENGLEWOOD CLIFFS, NEW JERSEY

A SPECTRUM BOOK

Library of Congress Cataloging in Publication Data

DUTTON, BERTHA PAULINE (date)
   The Pueblos

(A Spectrum Book)
Originally published as chapter 2, the Pueblo peoples,
in the author's Indians of the American Southwest.
   Bibliography: p.
   1. Pueblo Indians. I. Title.
E99.P9D79 1976   979'.004'97   76-15227
ISBN 0-13-740159-0

Cover photograph: A Navaho sandpainting (Photo by Michael Herion)
Drawing, page 1: Detail of a large Zuñi pottery bowl (Denver Art Museum: Cat. No. X-ZU-46-P)

© 1975, 1976 by Prentice-Hall, Inc.,
Englewood Cliffs, New Jersey

All rights reserved.
No part of this book may be reproduced
in any form or by any means
without permission in writing from the publisher.

Printed in the United States of America.

10 9 8 7 6 5 4 3 2 1

Prentice-Hall International, Inc., *London*

Prentice-Hall of Australia Pty, Ltd., *Sydney*

Prentice-Hall of Canada, Ltd., *Toronto*

Prentice-Hall of India Private, Limited, *New Delhi*

Prentice-Hall of Japan, Inc., *Tokyo*

Prentice-Hall of Southeast Asia Pte., Ltd., *Singapore*

CONTENTS

PREFACE   xi

ACKNOWLEDGMENTS   xiii

LINGUISTIC NOTES   xvi

the Pueblos

Brief History,   1
The "Privileged People" Myth,   4
Cultural Characteristics,   4
General Appearance,   7
Location and Population,   9
Languages,   10
Social Organization,   11
The Canes of Office,   12

THE TANOANS   14

Tiwa Indians,   14
Tewa Indians,   18
Towa Indians,   23

THE KERESANS   24

THE ZUÑIAN PEOPLE   33

THE HOPI GROUPS   36

Secret Cults and Societies,   42
Open Ceremonials,   59

CALENDAR OF ANNUAL INDIAN EVENTS   71

POPULATION FIGURES   77

BIBLIOGRAPHY   79

*This book
is respectfully dedicated
to
THE PEOPLE
. . . the original inhabitants
who revered this land
and its creatures
and strived to save and protect them*

.... PREFACE

The objective is to make this book generally readable for students, teachers, and travelers who desire knowledge, understanding, and authoritative information regarding the Southwestern Indians; it is for those who wish to know the basic features of Indian life, but who do not, perhaps, have the time or specialized training to read extensively of these various peoples.

"The changing Indian" is much more than an often heard phrase these days. The *changing Indian* is a fact, an almost incomprehensible fact. And changes are occurring at such a rapid pace that whatever one writes may well be out of date before the words are printed. Thus it can be said that this publication is already outdated in certain respects. However, the decade census of 1970 afforded a pivotal point, and the statements made regarding the Indian groups of the Southwest are comparable as of that time.

Throughout this work obvious changes are mentioned, and some of the more covert ones are noted. Although these may vary in kind and extent with the different Indian peoples, certain features in particular are undergoing alterations and transformations: education, living conditions locally and away from the home bases; labor opportunities, industries, economic exploitation, road works, soil treatments, dams and irrigation; health, welfare and social security; old ceremonies and new religions; and in some instances reappraisal of cultural values, appreciation of old mores, and intensification of self-esteem.

The writer has chosen diverse ways of presenting the information assembled; the material is too exhaustive for a book of this scope to be complete. Emphasis has been given to certain aspects of one culture, outstanding facets of another; some of the main features of specific organizations have been portrayed, and the complex and far-reaching traits of the Southwestern societies indicated.

No attempt is made to give equal attention to each and every cultural group. Rather, the design is to show that all of the aboriginal peoples fitted themselves to their particular environment and strove to live harmoniously with nature. To all, the land was sacred. An eminent place was given to the mountains and hills, to the water sources and streams; to the plant and animal life; to the sky above and the celestial bodies seen traversing it, and to the clouds that brought summer rains and winter snows. The individual and the group were linked unconsciously with their surroundings.

And thanks were rendered for the orderly progression of season after season and for the blessings received.

The very way of life itself gave rise to keen observations, philosophical thinking; myths, poetry, song, and drama, which treat of simple things or the majestic; grief and joy, lullabies and love, with diversity of melody and of text. Each of these merits studies by itself. Some of the poetic contributions of the Indians are included, and of non-Indians who have been inspired by them. Something of the philosophy, drama, and other manifestations of Southwestern Indian life will be found in the following pages.

Not infrequently, secondary sources are cited as well as original works. These may be available to readers who wish to pursue studies regarding the Indians; and many will refer to primary works not included with the references mentioned.

It is hoped that reading this book will aid in an appreciation of the first Americans and of their intelligent responses to the surroundings; of their developments and attainments; and then of their tenacious attempts to continue living according to their philosophy and judicious practices in the face of white colonization, conquest, and alternating procedures of the Europeans whose aggressiveness, missionizing and political ambitions, and material desires were so foreign to the Indian beliefs of proper conduct and rewards.

Simply recording brief facts of history and taking note of modern conditions—some of which evidence accretions and others diminutions—have made the consistency of pattern apparent and impressive: peoples came from Asia, slowly populated the Southwest (as well as all of the New World), adopted ways of life in keeping with the conditions at hand, and developed social organizations thus dictated, recognized the limits of their domain and the rights of others, and achieved their respective cultural patterns. Then came the outsiders.

Every conceivable means has been employed to overcome the indigenous peoples and their mores, to make them conform to the white man's way of life. Through four and a half centuries, these efforts have met with relatively little success. Indians may be made to dress like Anglos, eat their foods, dwell in their types of structures, adopt their means of transportation, follow their prescribed curriculums and business methods, undergo the missionizing endeavors of various sects, practice non-Indian forms of government, and the like, but no individual or no aggregate body whatsoever can make the Indian be different from what he *is*. He may change—if he sees fit—or he may mask his feelings and appear to accept the Anglo customs; but the circumstances which produced the people that came to be called American Indians and the centuries that afforded them time to develop a racial identity and distinctive social patterns made an immutable imprint.

Regardless of outside pressures the Indians have remained Indians, and they always will. It appears inevitable that their resolute spirit will bear fruit, now that their numbers are increasing; that their pride in the accomplishments of their people has been intensified; and that they are beginning to discern their existent capabilities and power, and their rights.

ACKNOWLEDGMENTS The preparation of this publication has extended over a number of years. Much of the research and writing was done during 1971. After that period no further research was pursued. However, as certain individuals undertook the reading of the manuscript several months transpired between its completion and submission to the press. Suggestions of the readers were incorporated: these include later information on occasion, and the addition of certain references and bibliographic items.

As this work took shape, I began to realize how much I owe to the mentors with whom I have been privileged to study, to many Indian friends who have guided my research and added to the knowledge and understanding of their cultures, to my anthropology associates and those in related professions, and to the institutions and foundations that have provided funds for travel and research opportunities and have printed my contributions.

I am most appreciative of the fact that several busy people have taken time to read this manuscript critically and offer advice for its betterment. Among these I give special thanks to C. Fayne Porter, teacher supervisor in language arts at the Institute of American Indian Arts in Santa Fe, who is also a well-recognized author of numerous published works. To teachers in the same school, I likewise give thanks: Michael H. Clark and Paul W. Masters. Colleagues in my profession who have been particularly helpful are Robert C. Euler, Grand Canyon National Park, Arizona; A. E. Dittert, Jr., professor of anthropology, Arizona State University, Tempe, Arizona; John Martin, associate professor of anthropology at the same institution; and Dorothy L. Keur, former professor of anthropology, Hunter College, New York. Although they have not read the manuscript, these colleagues have been very helpful:

Bernard L. Fontana, professor of ethnology, University of Arizona, Tucson; David M Brugge, Curator, Navajo Lands Group, National Park Service, Chaco Center, Albuquerque; and Robert W. Young, student and teacher of Navaho culture.

Within the Bureau of Indian Affairs and the National Park Service, many persons and divisions have supplied information by means of correspondence, telephone calls, printed matter and photographs. Those to whom I render special credits are: Charles R. Whitfield, agency land operations officer, Papago Indian Agency, Sells, Arizona; Kendall Cumming, superintendent, Pima Agency, Sacaton, Arizona; William S. King, superintendent, Salt River Agency, Scottsdale, Arizona; Stanley Lyman, superintendent, Uintah and Ouray Agency, Fort Duchesne, Utah; Espeedie G. Ruiz, superintendent, Ute Mountain Ute Agency, Towaoc, Colorado; José A. Zuñi, superintendent, Hopi Indian Agency, Keams Canyon, Arizona.*

Other persons to whom I am most grateful are Al Packard, whose wide knowledge of Indian arts and crafts has been drawn upon extensively; William Brandon, writer, who has supplied several pertinent articles which otherwise might have been overlooked; Lloyd New, director of the Institute of American Indian Arts, who has furnished information and publications; and Constance (Mrs. William A.) Darkey, Edith (Mrs. William D.) Powell, and Dr. Caroline B. Olin, who have given editorial aid.

For supplying source materials and miscellaneous data, I wish to thank the Navajo Census Office, the Northern and Southern Pueblos agencies respectively, the Jicarilla and Mescalero Apache agencies, the Hopi Tribe, the Zuñi Tribal Council, the Northern Pueblos Enterprises, and many other contributors.

To Fermor S. Church, I owe an especially great debt. Without him this publication would not have been undertaken and completed. His training in engineering (degree from Harvard University) and extensive knowledge of the greater Southwest, its peoples, and its problems—which results from years of teaching at Los Alamos, Santa Barbara, and Taos; from managing the Philmont Boy Scout Ranch; serving in high positions with electrical cooperatives for over two score years; and publishing scientific articles—complemented my learning and experience. Our discussions of matters about which I was writing and manner of presenting them added much to the significance of this undertaking. Some of the maps were prepared

*Location of individuals at time of supplying information.

by him: the majority are by Phyllis Hughes of the Museum of New Mexico staff.

As author of *Indians of the American Southwest,* I have drawn on many sources and have quoted material extensively. Permission to quote direct statements was sought, and outstanding cooperation received. Sincere appreciation is expressed to the following authors and publishers:

American Anthropologist, American Anthropological Association, Washington, D. C.
American Antiquity, Society for American Archaeology, Washington, D. C.
American Folklore Society, New York
Arizona Highways, Phoenix
The Arizona Republic, Phoenix
The Caxton Printers, Caldwell, Idaho
Columbia University Press, New York (through a daughter of William Whitman III, Mrs. Philip T. Cate, Santa Fe)
Diné Baa-Hane, Fort Defiance, Ariz.
Frontier Heritage Press, San Diego, Calif.
Indian Tribal Series, Phoenix
Institute of American Indian Arts, Santa Fe
Museum of the American Indian, Heye Foundation, New York
Museum of New Mexico, Santa Fe
Museum of Northern Arizona, Flagstaff
The New York Times
The Progressive, Madison, Wis.
Southwest Parks and Monuments Association, Globe, Ariz.
Southwest Printers, Yuma, Ariz.
Time: the weekly newsmagazine, New York
The University of Arizona (Dept. of Anthropology), Tucson
The University of Arizona (vice-president for business affairs and treasurer), Tucson
The University of Chicago Press, Chicago
The University of New Mexico Press, Albuquerque
University of Oklahoma Press, Norman
University of Washington Press, Seattle
Robert W. Young and *The Gallup Independent,* Gallup, New Mexico

Specific citations are given with the references and full data appear in the bibliography.

To those who contributed their photographic works I am deeply indebted, including the renowned Laura Gilpin, of widespread fame, and Elita Wilson, who has produced outstanding records of the Southwest and its Indian peoples. These, and most of the other contributors, gave their photographs gratis for use in this publication; in other instances museums and other agencies made their contributions without charge. The name of each photographer or source appears with the pictures.

Grateful appreciation is acknowledged to those who typed the final manuscript copy of this work from the rough drafts submitted:

Mary Jean (Mrs. Edward S.) Cook, Rebecca Brown, and Sharyn (Mrs. Kimball R.) Udall.

LINGUISTIC NOTES   In pronouncing Indian and Spanish words, *a* is soft as in "father," *e* as in "grey," *i* as in "machine," *o* as in "whole"; no silent vowels occur. The consonant *h* is silent; *ch* is sounded as in "church"; *j* is like *h* in "hay." In *ll*, the first *l* is lightly sounded and the second takes a *y* sound; thus *Jicarilla* is Heek-ah-REEL-yah.

As noted by a recognized linguist who has worked on Southwestern languages for many years, Professor George L. Trager, "It is customary to refer to a people by the same form for singular and plural (as 'the Hopi,' 'a Hopi,' etc.)."

As with the spelling of the term *Navaho,* some writers follow the Spanish use of "j," though the word is not Spanish, while the modern trend is to use the English "h."

Santa Fe, New Mexico   *Bertha P. Dutton*

the Pueblos

the Pueblos

BRIEF HISTORY   As the Spanish explorers during the sixteenth century pushed northward from Mexico, following ancient trails across desert wastes, over high mountain ranges and along flowing streams, the majority of indigenous peoples whom they encountered were those who had developed a sedentary life. When the Spaniards saw Indians living in compact, many-chambered, flat-roofed structures built around plazas, or squares, and from one to several stories in height with entering passageways, they were reminded of the villages of their homeland, hence they called each settlement a *pueblo*, and the "village dwellers" en masse were called "Pueblo Indians"—as opposed to nomadic or semi-nomadic peoples, or those on *rancherias*.

Through the centuries these Indians had developed cultures

based on hunting and gathering, to which horticulture was added in time. Stored food supplies provided for periods when products were not growing, and thus made it unnecessary for social units to move in search of food. With some 25% of their yearly food supply provided by horticulture, they were able to maintain increasingly larger groups and to attain a complex society. Theirs became an orderly way of life, with attention given to pertinent arts and crafts. Each pueblo or ranchería was established in relation to permanent springs or running water, and also to a close area having a considerable range of elevational gradients, within a short horizontal distance, which offered the maximum gathering potential. Near the villages were fertile gardens and fields where men and women shared their labors.

With the Spanish government taking formal possession of the Southwestern regions, Spanish saint names were given to the settlements. The Pueblo country was divided into districts and a Catholic priest was assigned to each. The Indians were required to take oaths of obedience and pay homage to the Catholic church and the Spanish crown.

At the pueblo of *Oke-oweenye* the Spaniards established the first capital of New Mexico in 1598, which they called *San Juan de Los Caballeros*. The next year, the Indian site of *Yunue-yungue* on the west bank of the Río Grande, directly across from the initial settlement, was chosen for the Spanish location, and this they called *San Gabriel*. It served as the capital until 1610, when the seat of government was moved to an old pueblo site which had been occupied centuries before, *La Villa Real de Santa Fe*, along the Río Sante Fe.

Becoming antagonistic toward the Spaniards who encroached upon their lands and forcibly altered their ways of life, the Pueblo peoples finally united in revolt and, in 1680, drove the invaders from New Mexico. (The name "New Mexico" as now applied appears to have been used for the northern province from 1582; the territory thus designated reached to the Pacific Ocean.) (Bloom 1940:106; *Carta Contenante . . . la Florida*) Twelve years of freedom from oppression were enjoyed until the Spaniards returned in 1692, under General Don Diego de Vargas and reconquered the northland.

Spanish rule continued until the Mexican Revolution of 1821, after which the Indians were declared citizens on equal basis with non-Indians. Life under Mexican authority, otherwise, was little changed for the Pueblos. Then the war between the United States of America and Mexico was fought, ending with the Treaty of Guadalupe Hidalgo which was signed in 1848. Mexico gave up all claim to territory east of the Río Grande (REE-oh GRAHN-day) and ceded New Mexico and upper California to the U. S. A., in return for payment of fifteen million dollars and other stipulations. Articles of the treaty provided for recognition and protection by the U. S. A. of Indian rights previously established under Spanish and Mexican rule.

Thereafter, title to Pueblo lands and those of the other Indian peoples were in question for decades. White settlers intruded upon Indian holdings in increasing numbers. In 1849 the Bureau of Indian Affairs (which had been created in the War Department in 1824) was placed under the newly established U. S. Department of the Interior, and the first Indian agent in New Mexico Territory was appointed.

According to a treaty signed on 30 December 1853—the Gadsden Purchase—the U. S. A. paid Mexico ten million dollars for all of the territory along the present southern boundary of this country, from the Río Grande to the Colorado River. Then, on 1 August 1861, all of New Mexico south of the 34th parallel was organized as the Territory of Arizona, with the boundary later to be changed as it is today. Six months before, formation of the Territory of Colorado reduced New Mexico in size, its northeastern section being included in Colorado.

Few of the pueblos could produce Spanish documents pertaining to their grants. The surveyor-general of the federal government took Indian testimonials in 1856 as to the holdings of some of the pueblos. Certain surveys were made in 1858, and a greater number the following year; these were confirmed by the Supreme Court and patents were issued to most of the pueblos in 1864, while others were not forthcoming until years later. About a half-dozen pueblos have less land today than they had according to the original patents, some have about the same, and the majority have received additional acres through various governmental actions and purchases.

New Mexico was admitted to the Union as a state in January of 1912. Twelve years later, Congress declared all Indians born in the U. S. A. to be citizens. However, the constitution of New Mexico excluded "Indians not taxed" from the franchise. Not until 1948 was legislative action taken which made Indians citizens of the state as well as of the nation, and thus entitled to vote. Arizona became a state of the Union approximately a month later than New Mexico; it had similar laws regarding the Indian residents, and took corresponding legislative action to give them the franchise at the same time as did New Mexico.

THE "PRIVILEGED PEOPLE" MYTH

Indians are not the privileged citizens that many people erroneously believe them to be. One fact widely misunderstood pertains to the relationship between Indians and the federal government. Let it be recorded here that:

The Federal Government makes no payments to a person merely because he is an Indian. Payments made to a person of Indian blood may represent income from his property collected for him by an agent of the United States. Other payments may result from compensation for losses incurred when lands are required in connection with Federal projects. Payments may represent the Indian's pro rata share of property belonging to the tribe of which he is a member. In each instance, money available for payments belongs either to the tribe or an individual and is held in trust by the U.S. Government. Therefore, Government checks are issued in making payments to individuals and to tribes. (Papago Indian Agency 1970:4)

CULTURAL CHARACTERISTICS

The Pueblos follow a communal pattern. Society is concerned with the group as a whole. Until recent times an individual got no recognition for his personal achievements; no ancient vessel or other work of art ever bore the name of its maker.

Living in this great uncrowded region, with day following night in orderly fashion, season after season, and where cataclysmic events were exceedingly rare, the Indian had two wonderful culture-forming assets space and time; space so that he could see things clearly, and time so that he could think and consider all matters carefully. The Indian had no system of writing; he could not jot down notes; and thus he had to remember everything and pass his knowledge on orally. Time and space and memory resulted in sound philosphy—which is reflected in all phases of the cultures which were developed in this area. No need to hurry or to make quick decisions. When some innovation occurred, it was thoroughly examined and discussed, and then rejected or accepted according to the unanimous decision of the group concerned. Changes, if made, were made slowly and for logical reasons.

The Indian, particularly the Pueblo, is restrained and affable, exceedingly polite. He wants to give you, or at least appear to give you, what you want. It seems to be a non-Indian tendency to ask leading questions, or "dumb" questions when seeking information, casual or serious. If one sees an Indian woman with a piece of pottery or a basket, or something else, and asks: "Did you make it?" the answer is likely to be yes, because she senses that is the answer desired. Should one question: "Who made that vessel? the answer might be: "my mother," or "my daughter," or "I did."

It should always be remembered that any Indian group, or even an Indian family, is now in a transitional stage. They are torn between their own ancient standards and those which are being urged or forced upon them by those of non-Indian culture.

Pueblo children have an active part in the social organization, in the family from the time of birth. A child sees and is a part of everything that goes on at home or in the plaza. From this constant participation, the manners of his people are learned early and completely. The association of a young child with those a few years older, "brings the individual at a very early age into the youth-controlled, socially accepted milieu of his own generation. (*See* Hawley and Senter 1946:142-143) Pueblo Indians think that a baby should be kept happy, for "when it grows up it will have many troubles." If a baby cries, it is given attention—picked up and entertained, not punished. If a baby cries for food, it is fed. When children are scolded, it is done quietly with low, controlled voice. Whipping is a form of punishment used when other measures have failed, but it is done in the privacy of the family only (excepting some ceremonial occasions).

Indian children are given and assume responsibilities at an early age; gradually they learn and participate in all phases of life which they will follow as adults. The boys are miniatures of their fathers, the girls of their mothers. Not until they take on more and more of the non-Indian cultures are the Indians confronted with problems of so-called juvenile delinquency.

Sexual standards among the Indians are different from ours, and may well be more realistic than those which we have long endeavored to maintain. Living in close association with other members of a family, children grow up knowing as much about sex matters as any other aspect of their culture. Premarital sexual experiments are common. They are not secret, but usually take place in the common sleeping room of parents and brothers and sisters. Pueblo adolescents usually were given sexual instructions by certain elders, so that girls and young boys suffered none of the stresses and strains and clandestine affairs to which non-Indian youth are subjected.

Traditionally, if a child is born out of wedlock, no stigma is attached to that child. The girl's parents usually raise it, and it takes a normal place in society. Certain it is that Indian youth have not suffered the physiological disturbances and oftentimes psychotic results that befall the youngsters of our society which has often failed to recognize adolescence as a distinct period when one is neither child nor adult.

The Pueblo Indians practice monogamy, whether they be married according to Indian customs or the ever-increasing civil and church ceremonies. Postmarital sexual infidelity is disapproved but is not uncommon. An erring wife, if caught, is usually punished by her husband, though a pueblo official may be sought for this purpose. Extramarital sexual relations are not uncommon either. Divorce, as well as marriage, is characteristically a family affair with the Indians. Among the Río Grande Pueblos divorce appears relatively rare; among the Zuñi it is more common.

Until modern patterns of life resulted in unbalancing the Indian economy and cultural mores and particularly in recent years of drought, wartime hardships, expanding economic, health and welfare programs, no Indian group failed to provide for its own orphans, old people, the ill and handicapped; and the group enforced punishments for infractions of its laws.

Most of the Pueblos, though they do not like death any more than we do, accept it for what it is, the end of man's material existence. It is the spirit which counts, and the spirit continues. A body is ceremonially prepared after death, dressed in traditional attire, and supplied with food, drink, and items of industry for use in the next world. Burial occurs as soon after death as possible, usually before nightfall of the same day of cessation of life. In its grave or cranny in the rocks, the body is watched for four nights, to keep away prowling dogs, coyotes, or other molesters. By then the spirit, it is believed, has reached the spirit world... and what happens to the earthly remains is of naught. Body orientation in burial is important among some of the Indians, while others appear to disregard the position of the corpse.

The Pueblos, like all other Indians, have taboos, avoidance practices, and other customs that they hold significant. Their reluctance to being photographed is not just a whim; it is a social matter with deep roots, and is related to sympathetic, or imitative, magic. If one has your likeness, he may exercise controls over you—usually to your detriment.

Gossip, criticism, and ridicule are major means of social control among the Indians. These factors tend to keep an individual from deviating from the norm of his culture. Indians are keenly sensitive to being singled out for public disapproval, laughter, or ostracism. They refrain from wrongdoing on the basis of such censure. Even where Christian training has spread to the Indians, the concept of postmortem reward or punishment has made little impression. Rather, they expect imminent and observable justice. For instance, if one does wrong, illness may befall his village or family group, a disastrous flood may destroy his property and crops, or severe drought may lay waste his season's efforts. It is much safer to observe the rules.

Indians feel that silence is part of the concentration that compels results. Speech, therefore, is restricted or taboo in certain ritual circumstances. The Pueblos have a profound conviction about the reasonableness of secretiveness. As long as one remains silent "his power is still in him." (Parsons 1939-I:433)

Even unto the present, some Indians regard long hair as "the badge of an Indian." It is considered by a man a necessary concomitant of his ceremonial life. As one Indian man put it: "When they cut [my hair], my heart hurt." Some were reluctant to have their hair cut, fearing they might be mistaken for Spanish-Americans, to whom they consider themselves superior. One of the most severe blows to many an Indian's status came when the armed services insisted on cutting the hair of adult Indian men. According to their mores, the kerchief is acceptable for Indian men to wear; hats are considered improper. Blanket wearing, like long hair, is another symbol of status. Moccasins are proper, whereas shoes are not. But with the demands of today we see all these less and less regarded. Conflicts result as acculturation progresses.

GENERAL APPEARANCE Understandably, the Pueblo Indians are not a homogeneous group of people. They reflect differing physical strains and admixtures. In general, they hold an intermediate position, not being of greatest stature or the smallest. They differ in head form and other respects, and fall close to the Indian mean. In the New Mexico pueblos,

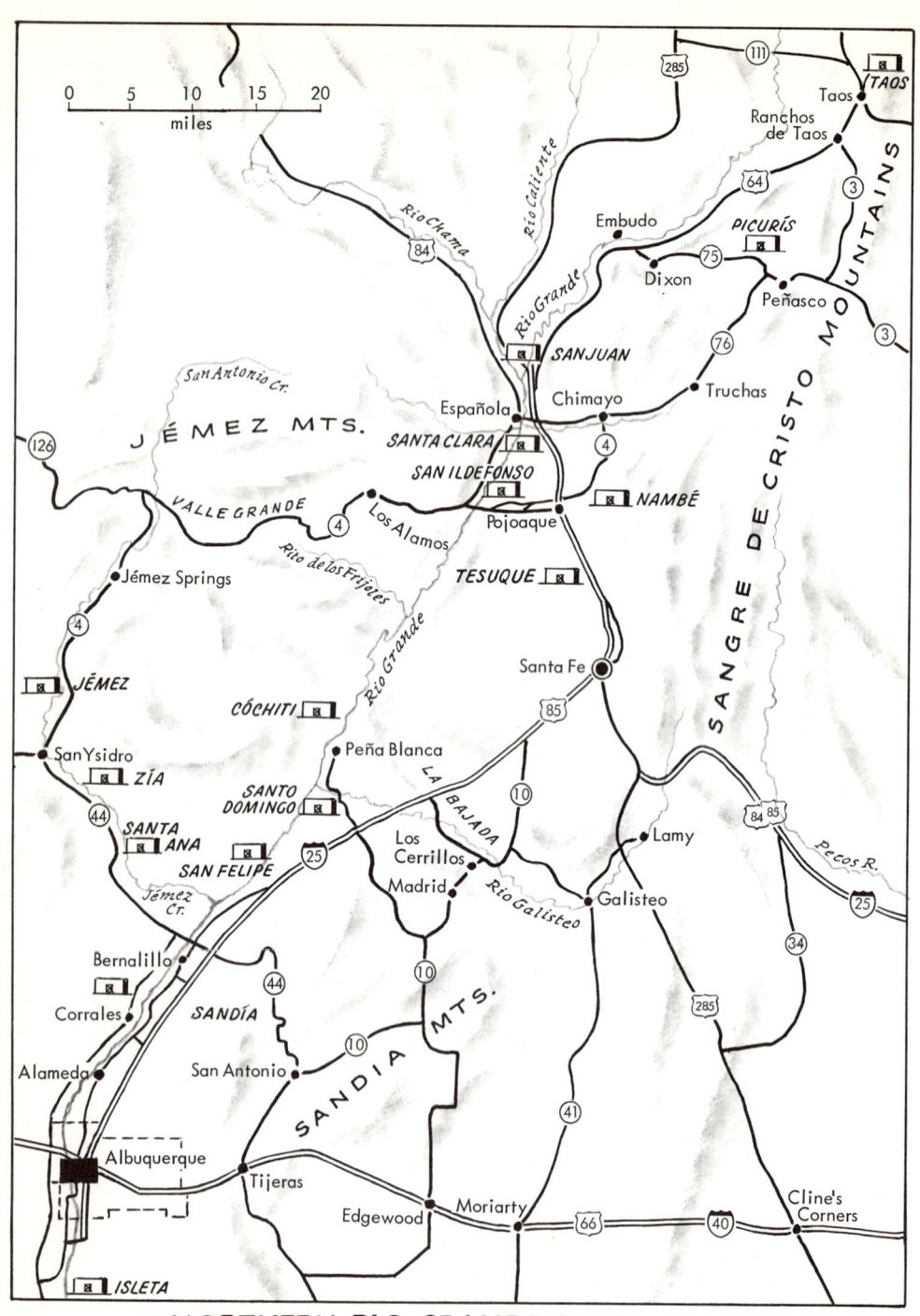

NORTHERN RIO GRANDE PUEBLOS, NEW MEXICO

where cereals long comprised the principal food-stuffs, a tendency to stockiness is observable, especially among the women whose lives center in the household. The Hopi (HOH-pee), who are the pueblo dwellers of Arizona, commonly are of small stature, due in part doubtless to their rigorous environment and basically strenuous life.

Usually the Pueblo peoples wear attire appropriate for homekeeping and farmer-stockmen activities. On festive occasions they have special clothing, either traditional or modern.

LOCATION AND POPULATION

Today, not only in their pueblos along the Río Grande and in Zuñi, southwest of Gallup, New Mexico, Pueblo Indians may be seen in and around the metropolitan centers of Albuquerque, Santa Fe, Taos and Gallup. One also may see Pueblo men, women, and children displaying their handicrafts in such public places as bus stations, airports, restaurants, hotels or motels, or museums; or they may have *ramadas*—temporary shelters—set up along the highways. In Arizona, the Hopi are much in evidence in the towns of Holbrook, Winslow, and Flagstaff.

As a matter of convenience, the pueblo dwellers of the Río Grande drainage are commonly spoken of as the Eastern Pueblos, while those of Zuñi and the Hopi villages are called the Western Pueblos. On occasion, Acoma and Laguna are included with the western peoples.

One sometimes sees Indians trudging down the roadway, perhaps signaling for a ride with a lifted hand or protruded lips. Or they may be riding. If on horseback, they take the softer footing along the fence that bounds the highroad, and one sees an unforgettable picture of profiles of dark skins and bright kerchiefs. A few years ago, a common sight was a family traveling to town in a farm wagon—perhaps a shiny one, its red and green paint reflecting good care, or an old one evidencing long use, its dished wheels making eccentric curves in the sand. Today, nearly all travel by automobile, some rusty and clunking, others bright and smart with a new paint job, or a late model station wagon or truck; the all-purpose pickup is favored by most.

Traces of the Pueblo past—scattered fragments of pottery, rock chips and worked stones, mounds of earth and rock, and crumbling walls that mark former villages—may be found on every hand. Great and small deserted dwellings and ceremonial structures falling into ruin, silent and impressive, also abound. One never escapes the consciousness of the centuries that these people have lived a vivid and constructive life upon this land.

The Pueblo Indians do not constitute a tribe as that word is understood by anthropologists and related researchers. Usually with them the term means something of this nature: "A tribe is a social group of a simple kind, the members of which speak a common dialect, have a single government, and act together for common purposes such as warfare." (Or *see* Hoebel 1958:661) A characteristic feature of a tribe is that it is a closed society (a group of individuals who have adjusted their interests sufficiently to cooperate in satisfying their various needs). (Eggan 1950:4) Its laws and morals apply to its members and not to outsiders. Each Pueblo group functions as an entity, each an independent lot of farming, house-building people, alike in some features and dissimilar in others.

New Mexico's Pueblo Indians in 1970 totaled approximately 29,335, and the number is slowly but consistently growing. The Hopi number a few more than 6,000. The chart on pages 271-73 gives the population of each of the pueblos and reservations, and these are located on the maps on pages viii, ix and 16.

LANGUAGES   The Pueblos, and all other Indians, may best be considered with view to the languages they speak.* For instance, the people of Taos (rhymes with house), Picurís (pee-kuhr-EES), Sandía (Sahn-DEE-ah), and Isleta (ees-LAY-tah) speak dialects of the *Tiwa* (TEE-wah) language.

On the reservations of San Juan (sahn HUAhn), **Santa Clara** (SAHN-ta KLAH-rah), San Ildefonso (sahn eel-day-FOHN-so), Pojoaque (poh-HWA-kay), Nambé (nahm-BAY), and Tesuque (tay-SOO-kay), the *Tewa* (TAY-wah) language is spoken. Tewa is also the language used at Hano in the Hopi country of northeastern Arizona, where some Pueblo Indians from the Río Grande valley migrated about 1700. Jémez (HAY-mez) is the only pueblo in which the *Towa* (TOH-wah) language is now used. Tiwa, Tewa, and Towa are related tongues that derive from a common linguistic family, the TANOAN, the parent stock being known as *AZTECO-TANOAN*.

The language of Zuñi, the westernmost pueblo in New Mexico, belongs to the ZUNIAN family, which appears to derive

---

*Linguists for the most part follow the J.W. Powell classification of Indian languages. Here, the editor adheres to this system of grouping Southwestern languages. (*See* Powell 1891:3-142 and Swadish 1967)

from the *PENUTIAN* stock. If true, ZUNIAN and TANOAN may be very distantly related.

Keres (KAY-rays) is spoken with dialectic differences in the other pueblos of New Mexico—in Cóchiti (KOH-chee-tee), Santo Domingo (SAHN-toh doh-MEEN-go), and San Fellipe (sahn fay-LEE-pay) along the banks of the Río Grande; in Santa Ana (sahn-TAHN-ah) and Zía (Tsee-ah) on the Río J́emez; and in the Laguna (lah-GOO-nah) and Acoma (AH-koh-mah) villages, roughly fifty miles west of Albuquerque. In general, linguists feel that Keres is quite distinct from any of the more inclusive language families of North America. Evidence indicates that the Keresans have been in the Southwest for a long, long time—as they say, "since time immemorial."

Excluding those who live in the pueblo of Hano, the Hopi Indians speak a single language, with several dialects, grouped under the UTO-AZTECAN family tree, of which nine branches have been identified as stemming from a Proto-Uto-Aztecan parent language spoken about five thousand years ago. (Miller and Booth 1972).

SOCIAL ORGANIZATION

Viewing the map on page 16, it is seen that loose geographic unity exists among the various linguistic groups. The northern Tiwa villages seem far removed from those of their kindred in Sandía and Isleta; considerable distance separated the eastern Keres from those of the western pueblos, Laguna and Acoma, and the dwellers in Hopiland are still further distant. What then makes these Indians seem to be one people and gives them the appearance of being a cultural unit? The answer undoubtedly is found in their attitude toward life as a whole, their religion in fact.

With the Southwestern Indians in general, and with the Pueblos in particular, religion transcends and permeates all else. It is the very core of their existence, day by day. All aspects of Pueblo life—the arts, crafts, industries, social structure, and religion—are inextricably interwoven, thoroughly integrated. From the simple tenet that *man must so live as to be in harmony with nature* ("nature's basic rhythm"), the Pueblo Indians developed a rich dramatic art—poetry, legendry, song and dance; by these means religion is given outward expression.

Sacred rites are performed in their fields prior to the planting, and appropriate ceremonies are conducted throughout the seasons—prayers for germination, growth, and maturation of the crops, and then thanks are given for prayers "answered and unanswered," as one old Indian has told it. Their hunts are ceremonially ordered and conducted, as are their salt gathering missions and other practices. Many of the designs on their pottery and other works of art are derived from motifs connected with their ceremonial life. Through religion all else is given significance; the lean or bountiful years are attributed to faulty or proper observance of religious retreats and rituals. No understanding of Pueblo life apart from its religious beliefs and procedures is possible.

Basically, each of the Pueblo communities is a closely united and highly systematized organization. Similar social patterns may be observed among the pueblos, yet great differences exist in regard to emphases upon certain organizations and practices. Some are meeting current stresses which the modern world puts on them by relaxing certain of their customs; others hold fast to their age-old strictures. Let it be kept in mind that the Pueblos are broadly alike, yet distinct. The people mingle, but hold apart. They do not favor marriage outside one's own village; while it may not be forbidden absolutely, it is often made difficult. The ceremonial dances are similar, but variations may be observed; these are important. Physical differences exist. Taos, for example, was the buffer pueblo on the north, receiving the brunt of raids by hunting tribes from the Great Plains, and its people exhibit a mixture of blood. Foreign elements show in traditions, societal practices, ceremonies, and in stature, wearing apparel, hairdress, and adornments.

Authority between the ecclesiastical leaders and those who serve in secular offices is sharply defined in each Pueblo group.

In the New Mexican pueblos, in accordance with a decree of the King of Spain in 1620, the secular officers' titles follow Spanish designations. In general these are a governor, two lieutenant governors, *alguacil* (sheriff), and *fiscales* (men who serve as church assistants—deriving from the office of prosecutor). These take office during the first week of January—usually on the first—and serve for one year, except at Isleta, Nambé, San Ildefonso, and Zuñi where the term of office is currently two years. Metal-topped canes inscribed with the Spanish cross became the badges of authority for the secular officers.

THE CANES OF OFFICE When Mexico won independence from Spain, sovereignty was successfully established and new staffs, silver thimbled, were presented to the pueblos, and the governors were authorized and commissioned to function in line with their long custom, having two canes each in symbolic support of the office. Ten years after the Gadsden purchase, President Abraham Lincoln ordered black ebony canes, silver crowned and inscribed with his signature, "A. Lincoln," for each of the then nineteen pueblos, extending the continuing authority and commission of the governors. Thus, in 1863, a third cane symbolizing the office under the new sovereignty came into possession of the pueblos in New Mexico.(Barton 1953; Faris n.d.)

The Spanish canes and the Lincoln canes bearing the name of a pueblo, the year, and the name of President Lincoln, are in evidence at any ceremony or gathering of the Pueblo Indians in any season of the year. Some of the pueblos have handed their Mexican canes over to the lieutenant governors; it appears that one or two of the villages have lost their Mexican canes and acknowledge having only two—the Spanish and Lincoln canes, as they are usually designated.

In 1883, Picurís lost the silver crown and ferule from its Lincoln cane. The stick was taken to an Indian Agent for replacement. Unfortunately, a heavier crown with paneled floral decoration was mounted, and an error was made in the date, showing the year as 1862. Pojoaque people lost the silver crown from their cane, having only the ebony stick left. But today, it is said that Pojoaque has a silver-headed, engraved cane. (Hayes 1971) Some of the canes are battered, but for the most part they are kept in fine condition. The respect for the pueblo canes is no less than is the congressman's respect for the mace in the U.S. House of Representatives.

In 1960, silver medals showing the profiles of Lincoln and President Dwight D. Eisenhower side by side, surrounded by the wording, "Republican Centennial, 1863-1960," were struck, fashioned into pendants, and strung on ribbons of red, white, and blue. Each pueblo governor was presented with one of these. They, with beribboned canes, serve as impressive symbols of office.

.... THE TANOANS

The Tanoan domain formerly extended widely from south to north and west to east. Tanoan social organization is characterized by strong dual organization, or dichotomy. In the northern Río Grande region, where the Tanoans now dwell, the two divisions—complementary ceremonial groups—are referred to generally as those of the north and south peoples, respectively, or as the summer people and the winter people. These divisions have been identified as moieties. (*See* Ortiz 1969:57-59, 73, 84, 108)

TIWA INDIANS   Of the Tanoan subfamilies, the Tiwa apparently were the initial Pueblo Indians to have entered the northern Río Grande. In prehistoric times Tiwa pueblos dotted the Río Grande valley from northern Mexico to the region of modern Albuquerque.

Usually overlooked in works on the Indians of the Southwest is a Tiwa group that dwells near University Park at Las Cruces, New Mexico. Commonly known as *Tortugas* (tor-TU-gahs), the official name of this village is Guadalupe Indian Village. It is controlled by an Indian corporation, *Los Indígenes de Nuestra Señora de Guadalupe*. An elaborate celebration commemorates the patron saint's day on 12 December, with activities the day preceding and that following the major event. The colorful ceremonies, influenced by long association with the Catholic church, include ritualistic singing, candlelight procession, pilgrimage to the summit of Tortugas Mountain, and dancing in front of the village church—all conducted under strict rules passed down by generations of Tiwa Indians, even though they now are Hispanized considerably. The number of those who may be counted as Indians today is unknown.

Although the Indians of the Southwest have the franchise after a hiatus of many years, and Indian people are taking their place in the legislative bodies, it is worth noting that, during the 1927 session of the New Mexico legislature, one of the Tiwa men of the Tortugas group served as representative from Doña Ana county. He was a diligent committee worker, and was frequently called to preside over the House of Representatives, a position which he filled with skill and dignity.

Throughout historical times, the other Tiwa have occupied

two locations. A northern group, of which the pueblos of Taos and Picurís remain, is separated by some 75 miles from their southern kinsmen who dwell to the north and south of Albuquerque, in Sandía and Isleta. Indians of the latter pueblos can readily converse with one another, as can those of Taos and Picurís; and the people of Sandía and Isleta can understand the dialects of Taos and Picurís, but the reverse is not true—Sandía and Isleta are understood by the northern Tiwa with difficulty. This suggests that the division occurred long ago and that the more isolated northern people have maintained the original character of their speech to a greater degree than have the others.

In the dual system of the Tanoans each division has, or had in the past, its own priest, or *cacique*. (The term *cacique* [kah-SEE-kay], is a Haitian word that was used extensively by early chroniclers to designate the priest-chiefs; it was incorporated into the Spanish language with this significance, and was added to the Indian vocabulary.) The cacique of the north, or of the summer people, has control during the summer, and that of the south, or winter people, during the winter. The cacique is the head of all pueblo organization; he holds office for life and has a staff as a badge of authority. The cacique, the kiva chiefs, and their appointees or selectees to the secular offices, constitute a hierarchial form of government.

At Taos and Picurís, six round ceremonial chambers are utilized. These are subterranean or semisubterranean rooms, built apart from the dwellings. Such a chamber is generally referred to as a *kiva* (KEE-vah), this being the Hopi name of a sacred ceremonial, assembly, and lounging chamber, characteristic of ancient and modern Pueblo settlements. "Kiva" embraces circular and rectangular structures of a specialized nature, whether they be built below ground or above, detached or among the houses. At Taos, each kiva is surrounded by a palisade of tall poles. Visitors are advised to keep a respectful distance from these. Paternal kiva membership is the pattern, but at Taos the choice of kiva is now optional, though the tendency persists for a father to "give" his child to his kiva or kiva cluster. The males are also the house owners.

In addition to its six kivas situated in the north and south segments of the pueblo—with a "chief" in charge of each—Taos has a seventh chamber of similar form which lies outside the village wall; it is sometimes described as "disused." Actually, it is used for retreats and prayers. Its original association was with a scalp society, or warrior cult, under the direction of the war chiefs. Picurís also has its structure designated as a scalp house, which undoubtedly has similar associations. Curing and healing were functions of the warrior society.

Formerly, if not at present, each Tiwa pueblo, as Taos today, had a race track as part of the village plan. Such tracks extend in an east-west direction, representing the courses of the sun and moon. Footraces are part of ceremonial ritual, being run to give power to travel to those celestial bodies. They represent contests between the north division of the pueblo and the south division. In the form of relay races, runners represent the north and south kiva groups, respectively; starting in the east, as the rising sun, they run to the west, touch another runner who races eastward, and so on until the winner is proclaimed.

Among the southern Tiwa the pattern regarding ceremonial structures is not so apparent. Inasmuch as deep subterranean chambers are known to have been in the region as long as a thousand years ago, it seems possible that the original kiva system may have been like that of Taos and Picurís. But Isleta and Sandía were in the main path of the Spanish *conquistadores*, and for over four and a quarter centuries they have been subjected to cultural disarrangements. The pueblos have been deserted, reoccupied after intervals of time, perhaps relocated, and admixtures of peoples have inhabited them.

The modern situation includes two rectangular ceremonial chambers built within the house blocks which are arranged about a central plaza. Isleta, largest of the pueblos in this group, has two rectangular kivas built among the dwellings and, in addition, a large circular chamber built almost wholly above ground and detached from other structures. It is a prominent feature of the architecture and is known as an "outside house." This is said to be used for maskless ceremonial dances, for painting the clowns, and for race ritual; it was primarily the place where scalps of enemies were kept.

At Isleta the divisions of the dual organization are known by the terms "Black Eye" and "Red Eye," respectively; everyone in the pueblo belongs to one or the other. Officers of the Red Eye (*Shúre*), or summer division, and the Black Eye (*Shifun*), or winter division, are prominent in the irrigation rituals and in certain maskless katsina dances; they direct the clowning, hunting and ball-playing, and other group activities.

In general, *katsinas*, or supernatural beings, are *not* impersonated by masked dancers among the Tiwa, although the small kiva groups make offerings to those personages.

Everyone belongs also to one of seven "corn groups" that hold winter and summer ceremonies for the sun; these signify seasonal transfer of official duties. An Isletan belongs to his mother's corn group. The corn chief, who may be referred to as "Corn Father" or "Corn Mother," serves as an intermediary with the curers, or expediter of deceased ones. The corn fathers and their helpers operate as a priesthood. The moon is regarded as "our mother moon," and stars are considered to be sons of the divine parents.

Isleta shows resemblances to both the Keres and Tewa systems. It has a cult of the dead, believing that weather and crop spirits dwell in the mountains. Their supernatural beings, like the katsinas of other pueblos, are impersonated in dances, but no masks are worn.

It is said that the office of cacique no longer exists at Isleta. Ritual matters are supervised by the war captain.

In 1947, this pueblo was the second in New Mexico to adopt a constitution to govern itself. In 1970 the document was replaced by a new constitution. All enrolled members of at least twenty-one years of age have the franchise. The top vote getter becomes the governor, the second is declared president, and the third highest, vice-president. A council is appointed, four members being named by the governor, and three each by the president and vice-president. The president is executive officer of the council, and the governor is chief executive of the pueblo. None of the elected officials receive a salary.

The pueblo of Sandía has two rectangular ceremonial chambers, although one is in disrepair. Here the division into summer and winter people is said not to exist; only one cacique holds office. He serves for life as the head of his people. The present cacique, of mid-age, succeeded an old man who had been in office since the 1940s. When choice of a cacique comes about, the privilege of naming him is traditionally rotated among the clans. The cacique appoints all secular officers annually. Directly under the cacique is an executive officer, the war chief, who also serves for life; he controls the nonsecular activities, supervising the keeping of rituals and the holding of dances. The governor works through the war chief in reporting on affairs of the pueblo—all business dealings. Five or six fiscales assist the governor in carrying out the dictates of the council, which is composed of former governors and war chiefs.

Sandía has been affected by influences of many peoples; perhaps as a result of this, the pueblo is said to have several matrilineal clans, "the number varying as some die out." (Hume 1970a) Corn groups like those of Isleta are evidenced.

With the Tanoan peoples, clan organization is generally nonexistent, or is weakly represented—indicating its adoption from neighboring Indian groups. A clan is recognized as a social group comprising a number of households, the heads of which claim descent from a common ancestor.

TEWA INDIANS Each of the Tewa villages in the upper Río Grande drainage is made up of small, loosely connected clusters of dwellings; their arrangement is irregular, with rooms generally offset, but they adhere to north-south and east-west axial lines. With growth, and possibly from long association with the Spanish-Americans—who customarily built their communities around plazas, and frequently enclosed sections within walls—the pueblo clusters came to assume plaza form, at least to a degree. In some instances, squares surrounded by structures are in evidence, in other cases the so-called plazas are only a matter of loose application of the word. Certain it is that little or nothing comparable to the compact buildings and courts of the prehistoric peoples of the Four Corners region, or of the Hopi pueblos of today, exists in the Río Grande Tewa villages.

The Tewa people live in five pueblos, all to the north of Santa Fe; in addition, some one hundred odd individuals of Pojoaque affiliation hold title to the Pojoaque reservation, and reside there or nearby. In each of these pueblos, dichotomy is of prime importance. Formerly, and to some extent today, a cacique presides over each division; Nambé, for example, has not had a cacique for several years. As with the Tiwa Indians, the summer cacique is in charge of the north people, while the winter cacique is in charge of the south people. Their office is for life.

The seasons are not evenly divided. Summer is considered to begin in February or March and to extend to November; winter lasts from November to February or March. Thus it appears that with the Tewa and Tiwa, and probably with all Tanoans originally, it is not the solstices that are of foremost importance in establishing the ceremonial calendar, but the seasonal transfer. The headman (cacique) of the north group gives the people to the headman of the south group in November, and the latter gives the people to the former in the spring. The winter solstice ceremonial is observed in January, while the summer solstice is celebrated in June. In matters of importance the cacique of the summer people has precedence over his counterpart.

Membership in the dual organizations is patrilineal, but the affiliation may be changed. A woman may join the division, or moiety, of her husband on marriage, or may remain as she is; the husband may transfer from one group to the other if he desires. It is the custom for each moiety to have a specialized, rectangular chamber built in the respective house blocks. The summer people are associated with the squash chamber, and the winter people with the turquois chamber.

In varying degrees the old ceremonial groups and moiety organizations of the Tewa pueblos are now broken down and their former distinct functions are mingled and confused. Traditionally, initiation into a moiety took place in a "big kiva." (*See* Hawley 1950:289) Today, San Ildefonso and Tesuque each have two moiety houses; the former also has a large circular chamber. In Santa Clara and Nambé the houses of the moiety chiefs are used in lieu of separate moiety rooms.

At Santa Clara the government is run under a constitution adopted in December, 1935, making this pueblo the first in New Mexico to adopt a constitution. This action was instrumental in healing a factional dispute that began in the late 1800s, when the then conservative ones of Santa Clara "were opposed to the acceptance of federal programs designed to upgrade the living conditions of the pueblo."

"The constitution effectively divided the secular from the religious, allowing the conservatives to concentrate on retention of the old religion and the young people to concentrate on the secular government." (Hume 1970b) The governing officials number six: governor, lieutenant governor, secretary, treasurer, sheriff, and interpreter. These are elected annually. The governor receives a nominal salary, and all officers receive expense allowances when on pueblo business.

It is said that the constitution divides the pueblo into four groups, two subgroups in each of the moieties, the summer and winter. Each of these groups can nominate candidates for any of the elective positions, and the candidates then run in a general election. Those eighteen years old have the franchise in regular elections, but on constitutional amendments the age limit is twenty-one.

Santa Clara's council is comprised of the elected officials plus two representatives from each of the pueblo's subdivisions. They have their own law and order setup, with a tribal judge whose decisions may be appealed to the pueblo council.

As is traditional with the Tewa, Santa Clara has a cacique at the head of its ecclesiastical organization. The position is for life.

Among the Tewa the extended family is emphasized, on both the father's and mother's sides. These large family groups often assemble in the home of some leader-member to discuss important matters. Clans, if they ever existed, have no significance today— although the term has frequently been used in speaking of various groups or societies. The simple family consists of a man and his wife and their unmarried offspring, or a widow or widower with children.

Heads of families, except old men and women, are responsible to the pueblo officials for such services as may be demanded of

---

A LULLABY OF NAMBÉ (Tewa)

Go to sleep,
Go to sleep,
Lest something come,
To take away
My little one.
So you must sleep,
My little one

From: *Songs of the Tewa*, by H. J. Spinden
©1933 by H. J. Spinden (Spinden 1933)

them. They may be called to clean the irrigation ditches, sweep the plaza before dances and feast day observances, and to perform ceremonial duties.

Patrilineal descent is the rule. House ownership is male, for the most part; and a tendency to build houses within a man's moiety seems evident. Originally, this created the basic architectural pattern.

At San Ildefonso, although a small pueblo numbering a little over 350, the outward evidence of past ceremonial organization is still manifest. The pueblo has two rectangular chambers, that of the winter people built in the northern most house block, and that of the summer people detached and in the southwestern part of the village. The large circular structure, built mostly above ground with an opening toward the southeast, appears prominently in the southern part of the pueblo. Entrance is by means of a stairway—formerly a ladder—leading to the top of the structure, where a hatchway gives access to the interior. The old ladder symbolized ascent from the underworld to a higher plane, or to an eminence. This chamber is said to be the oldest building in the pueblo; and it "belongs" to all of the people. It is used as a dance place. As at Isleta, this circular building is designated as the "outside house."

In certain of the pueblos, the war chiefs are also called "outside chiefs," and it appears that the outside house at San Ildefonso related to affairs of the warrior cult. The warrior society is no longer extant in the pueblo, although the paraphernalia is said to have been preserved.

Until a few years ago, the remains of a small, one-room building were observable on top of a low hill near the sacred spring of the west, of San Ildefonso. This was the chamber to which the old priest retired for his retreat.

The late William Whitman reported that the religious hierarchy at San Ildefonso is based on paternalism, and he stated that: "The Cacique is not a priest in the sense that he is an impersonation of godhead. He is 'father and mother' of the people, mortal as his children, whom in his wisdom he leads and directs. . . .To insure divine blessing it is believed that propitiation must be made not only by the priests (headmen) but by the group as a whole, and that through the efforts of the group, led and supplemented by those of the priests, the forces of nature are compelled to act in accordance with the needs of the people." (Whitman 1947:118*)

---

*Reproduced by permission of Marjorie Whitman Cate.

San Juan has two rectangular kivas built in the house blocks. The reader is referred to the extensive work of Alfonso Ortíz, himself an Indian, who dwelt in that pueblo with his family and has had unusual opportunity to study San Juan in detail. (Ortíz 1969) Santa Clara has two similar chambers, but detached from the dwelling structures. Tesuque has rectangular kivas built in the house blocks, and probably utilized two at a time; the pattern has become confused due to recent demolitions and rebuilding. At Nambé one finds only a large, circular structure in evidence. Archaeological excavations there exposed a small underground kiva, the floor of which was six feet below the present surface. It was twelve feet in diameter; it had vertical walls, the adobe plaster of which curved slightly at the floor level. The chamber was dated around A.D. 1400. The excavator observed that: "Small underground kivas used in prehistoric times as ceremonial chambers of religious societies, were replaced in most of the Río Grande pueblos by aboveground houses built for that purpose, or even by adaptation of one room in the house of the leader of the society." (Ellis 1964:38*)

The Tewa of Hopiland are mentioned later.

SONG OF THE SKY LOOM (Tewa)

Oh our Mother the Earth, oh our Father the Sky,
Your children are we, and with tired backs
We bring you the gifts that you love.
Then weave for us a garment of brightness;
May the warp be the white light of morning,
May the weft be the red light of evening,
May the fringes be the falling rain,
May the border be the standing rainbow.
Thus weave for us a garment of brightness
That we may walk fittingly where birds sing,
That we may walk fittingly where grass is green,
Oh our Mother the Earth, oh our Father the Sky!

From: *Songs of the Tewa* by H. J. Spinden
© 1933 by H. J. Spinden

---

*Reproduced by permission of the Society for American Archaeology, from *American Antiquity* 30:38 (1964).

TOWA INDIANS

The pueblo of Jémez is the remaining member of a third Tanoan subfamily, the Towa. It is located on Jémez Creek, or the Río Jémez, west of Santa Fe in the mountains of the Jémez range. Seventeen survivors from the pueblo Pecos moved to Jémez in 1838, and descendants of Pecos parents and the Jémez people are presently enumerated together. Being located quite apart from the Tiwa and Tewa peoples, but close to non-Tanoan villagers, Jémez displays many characteristics which are attributable to the Keresans.

There are two large rectangular kivas, but the dual organization has broken down, although summer and winter people are recognized; no moiety houses exist. Society houses occur in the regular house blocks. The Jémez developed clans, with descent reckoned through the maternal line. One has to marry outside the clan. Clans play but a minor part in the economic and ceremonial life of Jémez. Weakness of the clan system probably reflects a borrowed trait, or a marginal occurrence. House owning rests with the males for the most part.

One cacique serves for life; he possesses a "Mother" fetish. The cacique is assisted by two men who are probably relatable to the war chiefs of old. Foremost duty of the cacique is to watch the sun, that is, to determine the arrival of summer and winter and set dates for ceremonies accordingly. Races of the kick-stick type are held on a north-south track.

.... THE KERESANS

The origin of the Keresan people is unknown. One linguist subdivides them into four groups: Acoma and Laguna, Zía and Santa Ana, San Felipe and Santo Domingo, and Cochiti. He says that Acoma and Laguna, usually considered as the western Keres, "have had a history of linguistic development independent to a certain degree of the other dialects," (Davis 1959:78) that is, of the eastern Keres. Acoma and Laguna also have distinct histories extending into prehistoric times. (Davis 1959:83*) Some evidence of a closeness between the language of Zía and the western Keres has been detected. (Spencer 1940; Hewett and Dutton 1945:19) And viewing the maps it is seen that the eastern and western villages share a continuity of terrain. Keres people have demonstrated a preference for locating their pueblos atop eminences, usually lofty sandstone mesas above the valley lands. Trails led directly between the two regions; and pueblo ruins now existing may have been occupied by Keres people.

Archaeological investigations indicate that those who now occupy the Keres districts have been there for a very long time. Like the Tanoans, their former territory well may have been more widespread.

One belief, although remote, is that the Keresan language may be of HOKAN-SIOUAN affiliation, suggesting that the Keres represent an intrusion of peoples who pushed into the Southwest around 4,500 years ago—thus being descendants from Archaic peoples (Sapir 1929; Dittert 1959; Eddy 1965:24) who came from a southerly direction and merged with northerly ones. Such a position and history of the Keres would be in harmony with the finding of Strong, (Strong 1927:57) who believed that certain peoples, including a Yuman-speaking enclave, pushed themselves into what had previously been a continuous Azteco-Tanoan domain.

Regardless of their origin and regional developments, the Keres display cultural features that differ in varying aspects from those of the Tanoans. Acoma was established at or near its present location as early as A.D. 900, and its occupation has been continuous since 1075. (Dittert 1959) Its structures are built in parallel rows of

*Dr. A. E. Dittert, Jr., recognizes these two peoples as distinct in central western New Mexico for at least 4,500 years.

terraced house blocks, tending in an east-west direction; all face toward the south. Among the dwellings, seven rectangular ceremonial chambers are situated on the ground floor. The head kiva differs from the other six in having a floor vault over which a plank is placed, acting as a resonator when used as a foot drum.

Contrary to Tanoan organization, with the Keres peoples clans are, or were, of foremost importance. Each Acoma Indian is born into his mother's clan. These clans are exogamous; that is, one must marry outside his clan, and so the chief function of the clan is to regulate marriage. Descent is reckoned in the maternal line, and houses are property of the women. The economic unit is the household. Although the part that clans play in ceremonies and general pueblo procedures may now be minor, in olden times the clan heads owned fetishes, settled disputes between members, went into a series of summer retreats for rain, assisted the medicine societies—particularly during the winter solstice observance—and conducted ceremonies relating to supernatural ones associated with the clans.

Only one cacique holds office at Acoma, and he represents and cares for the whole pueblo, reflecting lack of dichotomy, or dual organization. The cacique is the highest religious officer and the political head of the pueblo; his most important ceremonial function is to watch the sun and determine the solstices; he sets the date for practically all ceremonies. Here, as with the Azteco-Tanoans, the sun is recognized as representative of a supreme deity.

Laguna was without ceremonial chambers for many years. Formerly, two rectangular ones were built aboveground, one on the east side of the village and the other at the west end. The east kiva was the repository for all of the paraphernalia belonging to the warrior society, which performed the scalp dance. The west kiva housed all ritualistic property of the katsina cult. Children joined the kiva of the father, and wives that of the husband.

A few years ago, a new chamber was constructed at Laguna, in the southwest part of the pueblo, and this is being called a kiva. It is said to be "all modern."

At Laguna, one cacique was chosen for life; he spent his time in prayer and sacrificed for the welfare of his people. The cacique was assisted by war chiefs, representing twin war gods; they were concerned with warfare, hunting, and guarding the people and the rituals. They were aided by chiefs' helpers.

Laguna followed a matrilineal-matrilocal pattern of organization, with exogamous clans bearing totemic names; they had ceremonial, judiciary, and economic functions. For many years, two groups—one conservative and the other progressive—have been observable at Laguna.

A degree of unanimity is found in the organization of the eastern Keres pueblos, but their social pattern differs considerably from that of the western peoples, and from the Tanoans with whom they are in proximity. As a rule, the Keres did not live east of the Río Grande. Generally speaking, their settlements were on the west side of that stream, and their domain extended no farther than the eastern mountains which border the Río Grande valley, that is, the Sandía range and the Ortíz-San Pedro mountain group.

Today, five pueblos are extant among the eastern Keres: Cochiti, Santo Domingo, San Felipe, Santa Ana with outlying farming communities, and Zía. Whether large or small, each pueblo has two round ceremonial structures built above ground and apart from the dwellings. One of these is associated with summer (squash) people and the other with winter (turquois) people. Each kiva group is associated with particular clans, and with certain medicine societies—thus involving a triple organization.

The spiritual leader, the cacique, in the larger pueblos is appointed by the war chief for life; he has to be a member of a particular society (Flint), and he is associated with a "clown" group. In no instance is the clan organization strong. It follows matrilineal descent for the most part, clan exogamy, and matrilocal residence. In the pueblo of Zía, however, clans display patrilineal descent; matrilocal residence is followed for a while, then the groom builds a new home for occupancy.

Because of the prominent two-kiva system, relating to seasonal divisions made manifest by the occurrence of the winter and summer solstices, and in view of the ceremonies relating to each season, a general dichotomy in the social organization prevails. This has been identified as a moiety system by some investigators. Keresan society is better considered as clan-based, although the clans now function but weakly. Then, realizing the seasonal divisions and accepting the probability of influences from the strong Tanoan dichotomy system, it is possible to visualize an original Keresan pattern quite diverse from that of their neighbors. The Keres evidence a complicated social structure, embracing clans, kiva groups, and medicine societies. Under the control of its single cacique, each Keres pueblo in the east has two circular ceremonial chambers built apart from the dwellings, while in the west these are rectangular, built among the house blocks, and may number two or more. All are aboveground structures.

Fig. 1 A Taos war dancer. His attire was adopted from the Plains Indians (the feathered war bonnet is not native to the Southwestern Indians). The drummer, who provides the dance rhythm with a single-headed drum, wears his hair in the style of the northern pueblos of the Tiwa and Tewa groups. The beaded moccasins are also typical of the Plains Indians.

Photo by Elita Wilson

Fig. 2 A dance team from the eastern Keres pueblo of Santa Ana enacts a buffalo dance at an off-reservation celebration. The dance leader is at the left; a drummer stands behind the buffalo maiden. Each buffalo dancer wears a painted buckskin kilt, with tin tinklers at the bottom edge; the waist is encircled by a red textile belt and band of bells; strings of shells are wrapped around the wrists and armbands adorn each arm. A gourd rattle is held in the right hand and a feathered bow in the left; the neck-chest ornaments are fashioned of shells, tied down to hold them secure during the highly animated movements of the dance. A real buffalo head with horns is worn as headdress.

Photo by Elita Wilson

Figs. 3 & 4   A Hopi woman making *piki*. *Left*, putting batter on a stone griddle with a whisk of her hand; the batter is in a Hopi bowl. *Right*, removing a sheet of paper-thin bread from the griddle; she places it in a Hopi basket, layer on layer.

Photo by Suzanne de Berg

Fig. 5   A pottery bowl is molded into shape by a Hopi woman from First Mesa, Arizona.

Photo by Suzanne de Berg

Fig. 6 A Hopi woman placing rods for the foundation of a basket. Fibers are kept pliable in moist sand.

Photo courtesy Elita Wilson

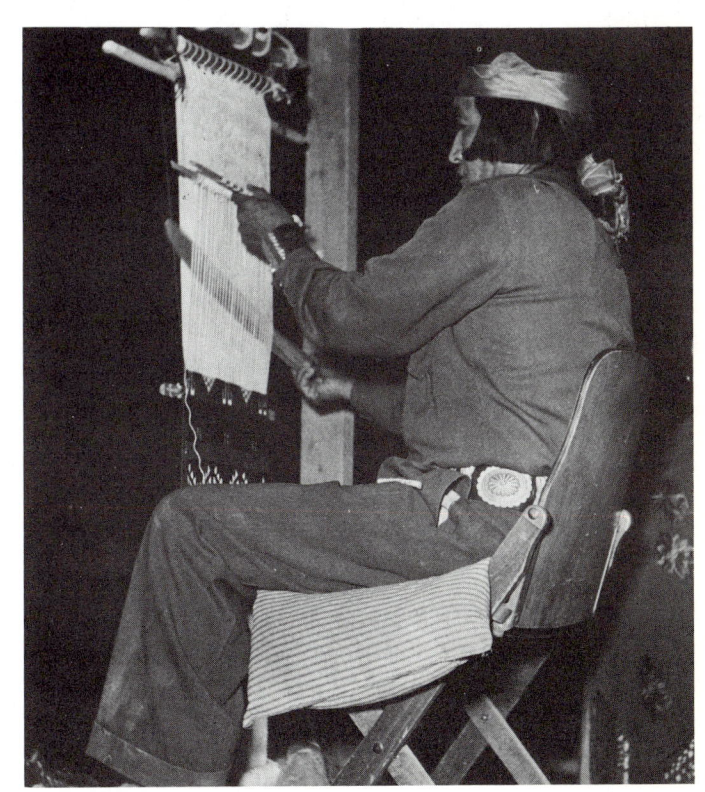

Fig. 7 A Pueblo man from Hopiland, with hair cut at sides only and worn chongo style. He is weaving a ceremonial sash; the decorated portion is in brocade weave, showing a conventionalized katsina mask, Broad Face. Note the moccasins he wears.

Photo by Elita Wilson

Fig. 8 Hopi men painting katsinas in a chamber decorated with Navaho rugs and a large double-headed drum. The figure between them is the highly favored *Hémish* katsina, a potent fertility figure. Men properly attired are commonly chosen to represent these personages at the Home dances that close the ceremonial season, when "the gods" go to their home in the San Francisco peaks in late summer.

Santa Fe Railway photograph, Elita Wilson Collection

Fig. 9 A Nightway depiction dating from soon after the Pueblo Rebellion of 1680. On display at the Museum of Navaho Ceremonial Art, Santa Fe.

Photo courtesy Harry L. Hadlock

Fig. 10 A rectangular kiva built among dwellings at the pueblo of Jémez. Red chili is drying on the *viga* ends. A closed conical oven is seen at the angle of a house and the ceremonial chamber (which is entered by means of two tall ladders).

Photo by B. P. Dutton

Fig. 11 The pueblo of Taos, north plaza, with Mount Wheeler (the highest elevation in New Mexico) in the background.

Photo by B. P. Dutton

Fig. 12 The Hopi often set up equipment for outdoor living during the warm days, as seen here at Upper Moencopi.

Photo by B. P. Dutton

.... THE ZUNIAN PEOPLE

Archaeological and linguistic evidence indicate that Zuñi-speaking people have been in their present location for some eight hundred years, or more. And it appears likely that Indians traveled between Mexico and the regions to the north for centuries; no boundary existed until the time of the Gadsden Purchase. In the 1530s, verbal accounts concerning Indians of the unexplored lands of the Greater Southwest reached the ears of the Spanish conquerors in Mexico. By 1535 they had heard of many-storied houses built of stone and adobe, in which the Indians dwelt. Don Antonio de Mendoza, the Spanish viceroy, soon became interested in the opportunity of adding new territory and expected riches to the empire of Charles V, and of Christianizing the Indians. Accordingly, a Franciscan friar, Marcos de Niza, was sent forth at the head of an exploring party, in the spring of 1539.

Among a group of Piman Indians—the Sobaipura (so-BAI-pu-rah) who occupied the Río San Pedro and the Gila valleys until about the end of the eighteenth century—Fray Marcos met the first Zuñi Indian of whom specific mention is known. The old Indian told the friar of the pueblos of his homeland and of neighboring peoples. He was the original informant concerning Hawikuh, or *Ahacua*, which he described as the largest of the Zuñi pueblos.

Fray Marcos sent a member of his party, a black man named Estevan (es-TAY-vahn) de Dorantes, ahead with a few companions to scout the way to Zuñi and to pacify the Indians. Estevan is credited with having had a gift for dealing with strangers, but his reception among the Zuñi was anything but friendly. The Indians refused his entrance to Hawikuh; they stripped him of his possessions, sent him forth, then fell upon and killed him. Some of the party escaped and took word back to the friar, who retreated to Mexico. Another explorer, Francisco Vasquez de Coronado, entered Zuñiland the following year (1540).

Aside from the Estevan incident, the Zuñi, like the Pueblo Indians of the Río Grande, were friendly toward the Spaniards when they first entered the region. Other explorers and missionaries came and went; some of the latter were admired and respected by the Zuñi, others stirred resentment which caused their dispatch. The Zuñi took part in the Pueblo Rebellion of 1680, although they were less involved than were the Río Grande Pueblos, who were closer to the scene of the uprising. When Vargas effected his reconquest in 1692, he found the Zuñi withdrawn to the eminence called *Towayalane*, or Corn Mountain. Shortly thereafter, they began the building of their present pueblo, including the old site of Halona on the Zuñi River.

Currently, most of the Zuñi people live in that pueblo; a few have permanent dwellings in nearby settlements. The lands of Zuñi were not recognized by executive order of the U.S. government until 1877. The boundaries then established were amended by Presidential order in 1883 and again in 1885. The reservation now covers some 440,000 acres to the southwest of Gallup, New Mexico. Zuñi is one of the most populous of the Pueblo groups, numbering around 5,640 Indians. Nonresident Indians increase the population by several hundred, making about 6,000 in all.

Traces of a dichotomous organization have been detected at Zuñi, with recognition of north people and south people, or summer and winter people. The summer cacique is considered to be speaker to the sun, and the winter cacique, rain priest of the north. Clans are of considerable significance, although as such they have no social or political functions. They number about thirteen, are totemically named, each being composed of one or more unnamed lineages; they are exogamous. Both the mother's and father's lineages are important; their social and ceremonial duties are differentiated sharply. Formerly, the clans were grouped into phratries, that is, major groups including a number of clans, which were associated with the six directions—the cardinal points, the zenith and nadir. The economic unit is the household, normally composed of an extended family based on matrilocal residence—occupying a series of adjoining rooms which are owned by the women, since descent is matrilineal.

It has been noted that an individual is "fitted into an intricate and closely knit social organization." Also, "The elementary family, so important elsewhere, is merged into the household group, and the specific roles of relatives are affected by their position in the social structure. A Zuñi is born into a certain household, which determines his clan affiliation and kinship status, and, in part, his future ceremonial roles." (Eggan 1950:191*) Ritual activities are primarily in the hands of the father's household, while economic activities are primarily in the hands of the mother's household and lineage.

*Copyright 1950 by the University of Chicago Press. All rights reserved. Reproduced by permission.

Zuñi has an elaborate ceremonial organization centering in six kiva groups (one for each direction), associated with medicine societies and an extensive esoteric cult (*kóko*) and priesthoods—all of which cut across clan and household groupings. The kivas, like those of the western Keres and the Tanoans, are rectangular and aboveground; some are built in the house units, others are detached. Sacred fetishes are in the care of the women and their brothers. On ritual occasions the men return to their natal household to carry out important ceremonial duties. Medicine societies are not tied in with the kiva system.

The Zuñi people, perhaps more than most of the Río Grande Pueblo groups, have maintained their social organization insofar as has been possible in the face of inevitable change. In recent years, isolation of the pueblo has ceased. Improved roads and pavement, modern vehicles, public utilities, development of resources, and government projects of varied types, have brought the Zuñi into cultural ferment, slowly but surely. Education has been available on the reservation since 1882, first through the primary grades only, then through high school since 1956. Over 80 percent of the Zuñi who have been graduated from high school have continued in commercial and vocational schools and/or in colleges.

Alert officials at Zuñi became aware of a federal law of 1834 which had never been used, but which allowed Indians to administer their own reservations with the approval of the Secretary of the Interior. The Zuñi Tribal Council held a ratification election on a proposed constitution to replace custom laws which had been followed for centuries. All registered tribal members over twenty-one were allowed to vote, and they favored the change to home rule. Currently, eighteen-year old Zuñi people are allowed to vote.

Formal agreement by which the Zuñi took over direction of the federal agency on the reservation was signed on 23 May 1970. This agreement was the culmination of a comprehensive development plan that had been worked on for a period of years. The plan contains forty-three programs, with the major goals of increasing individual income, enhancing educational opportunities, and improving living conditions. The agreement is described as being flexible; it can be canceled by either of the signing parties on 180 days written notice if it does not work out. By taking this impressive action, the Zuñi became the first tribe in the nation to take control of its own affairs. The council was presented the first Interior Department Indian Leadership Award for its initiative.

THE HOPI GROUPS

The Hopi, the pueblo dwellers of Arizona, have occupied their domain for over a thousand years. The designation *Hopi* is abbreviated from *Hopituh Shi-nu-mu*, which means "the peaceful people." For the most part, their villages are perched atop three high, barren mesas located northwestward from Keams Canyon, where an Englishman, Thomas V. Keam, started a trading post in 1878. The federal government established offices there in 1887, Keam's holdings being purchased and made part of the headquarters. From there, the mesas were called "First Mesa," "Second Mesa," and "Third Mesa," going from east to west. This was just opposite to the order in which the Hopi themselves regarded their highland sites.

In ancient times the location of the Hopi settlements on the three southern prongs of Black Mesa served as a natural protection from enemies. The dissected highland, some sixty miles in diameter, is drained by streams that carry sand and silt southward to the lower plain. There the prevailing southwest winds separate the soil materials and blow the sands back to form large dunes. These absorb the water and lessen the runoff when rains fall. Permanent springs thus result.

The villages on these mesas, like those of the Río Grande pueblos, have an intricately interwoven social structure. They have never had a tribal government of any kind. Each village has its own organization and each individual has his own particular place in the operation of his community. The clan system is basic; it is matrilineal and matrilocal, resulting in blocks of houses built adjacent to the home of the matriarch. The clan is stronger among the Hopi than elsewhere among the Pueblos; and a strong clan system correlates with a weak political system. (Eggan 1950:117-118) It has been stated that to a casual visitor in a Hopi village, "its government is so lacking in form as to seem almost nonexistent." (James 1956:107*) Nothing of a dichotomous organization is to be seen. The household is the economic unit; labor is judiciously divided between the men and women. Each major clan has a fetish which is kept in the clan house and is presided over by the woman considered to be the clan mother.

*Reproduced courtesy of the Caxton Printers, Ltd.

Women own the houses, food, seed for the next year's planting, the springs and cisterns, and the small irrigated gardens that they work. The men do the herding, hunting, and farming away from the village. They gather and haul the fuel, and theirs are the duties of spinning, weaving, and moccasin making—all of which are becoming less and less evident today. Married men live in the household of the wife, but they continue association with their mother's and sisters' homes—their "real homes"—and participate in ceremonial activities of the family clans.

The Spaniards visited Hopiland, or old Tusayan, under Don Pedro de Tovar, a lieutenant of Coronado, and occupied a village believed to have been the now ruined *Kawaiokuh* (kah-WAI-oh-kuh), from which the Indians had fled at the approach of the small party of armed invaders. The first contact between the Spaniards and Hopi followed—a friendly encounter apparently, for the Indians brought gifts and Tovar assembled his men in a camp near the pueblo. There, the Spaniards learned of a great river flowing in a deep canyon—the Colorado River of present days—and Don García de Cárdenas was ordered to search for the mighty stream, which has always played a major part in Hopi mythology. For forty years the Hopi were not again visited by the Spaniards.

In 1583, Antonio de Espejo and a few soldiers passed through the Hopi towns. They spent several days in *Awatobi* (ah-WAH-toh-bee), now in ruin a few miles east of Walpi (WAHL-pee), and in other villages. The Indians were cordial and gave the Spaniards many presents before Espejo continued on, seeking gold (but finding silver). Juan de Oñate visited Tusayan in 1598 and in 1604. From 1629 until 1680, Franciscan missionaries tried to convert the Hopi to Christianity. Missions were established at Oraibi (oh-RAI-bee), Shungopovi (shung-OH-poh-vee), and Awatobi. (Montgomery, Smith and Brew 1949; Smith, W. 1952 and 1971) The period was one of great unrest among all of the Pueblo peoples; their priests resented the Spaniards' interference with the native religious ways; they chafed under the enforced labor demanded of them; and they deplored the ravishing of their women. Distrust and unfriendliness toward the intruders grew and intensified.

Like the Río Grande Pueblos, those of Tusayan were ripe for rebellion, and they joined in the uprising of 1680. They killed four friars and demolished the churches and outlying *visitas*. Vargas, in 1692, was in Tusayan and gained some submission from the Indians; Oraibi did not give obeisance, for Vargas did not visit that village. The Spanish reconquest meant little to the Hopi. Their isolation and the aridity of the region did not attract Spanish colonists. From those days, nearly three centuries ago, Spanish influence has faded into history.

Settlements have been moved. Shungopovi people went atop the second, or "Middle Mesa," and built a new pueblo in 1680; and those of Walpi moved to the tip of First Mesa after 1700. Following the Pueblo Rebellion, Tano Indians (Tewa from near Abiquiu in New Mexico), who wanted to escape the vengeance of the Spaniards who they feared would return to their pueblos, were invited to establish a village at Hano (HAH-noh)—as THAN-noh was pronounced in the western region—and serve as guards at the top of the trail. Hano and Sitchumovi (seet—CHEW-moh-vee), which was built in the 1700's as an overflow from Walpi, make the First Mesa structures appear almost continuous.

A new pueblo, Shipaulovi (shee-PAUL-oh-vee), was founded in its present location on Second Mesa, and Mishongnovi (mee-SHONG-noh-vee) was moved to the end of the mesa from a lower site near the Corn Rock shrine (originally two imposing sandstone pillars, now one has fallen).

A farming settlement was set up along Moencopi Wash in the western part of Hopiland by Chief Tuba, in 1870, and Upper and Lower Moencopi (MOH-en-koh-pee) came into being. A short distance from there, a government agency established by Mormon missionaries and named for Chief Tuba, or *Toovi*, from Oraibi, has become Tuba City. The Mormons hoped to produce woolen textiles on a large scale and founded a woolen mill there in 1879—a venture which was short-lived. The Mormons believe the American Indians to be descendants of the "lost tribes of Israel," so they feel obliged to treat them in a friendly manner. Their efforts to convert the Hopi have been but mildly successful.

Old Oraibi has occupied the same locale since about 1100; it vies with Acoma as being the oldest continuously inhabited village in the nation. It was one of the largest of the Hopi towns until 1906, when dissension brought about the founding of Hotevila (now more commonly spelled Hote-villa, but pronounced hoh-tah-VILL-ah), then Bacabi (BAH-kah-bee) in 1907, and New Oraibi (1910) on Third Mesa. (Cf. Coze 1971:4)

During the first quarter of the nineteenth century, Americans were visiting the Hopi country in steadily increasing numbers— explorers and trappers, soldiers and surveyors, traders and missionaries, government agents, and others. In 1853, the villages were ravaged by smallpox, an introduction of the white man. Lieutenant A. W. Whipple of the Topographical Engineers reported that at one pueblo he found "only the chief and one other man remained of all the able-bodied men of the town." The living dragged the bodies to the edge of the mesa and threw them over the cliffs. This cut the Hopi population drastically, as did another epidemic around 1892.

Hopiland was part of the U.S.A. for about twenty years before an agent was assigned to take over supervision of these Indians, in 1869. A year later a Protestant group established a mission school at Keams Canyon; like other attempts to convert the Hopi the results were negative. Their age-old religion provided security for the Hopi and their way of life—the "Hopi Way"—satisfied their needs.

A Mennonite preacher, H. R. Voth, without approval of the Oraibi people (but with the consent of government officials) built a stone church on the mesa near the pueblo in 1901. It stood as an "offensive eyesore" until it was struck by lightning and gutted by fire in 1942. (James 1956:30) The ruin may be seen as one passes along the roadway a short distance from the pueblo.

When conditions became more settled, some individuals began moving to ranches on the lowlands, generally south of the mesas; others went to places such as Keams Canyon, where many work for various governmental divisions in numerous capacities, or to Polacca built below First Mesa, to Moencopi or Tuba City. Perhaps 1,200 work in more distant communities—Holbrook, Winslow, Flagstaff, and Grand Canyon or elsewhere. But most of these wage earners will be back in their hereditary homes on the mesas for the seasonal ceremonies. In these modern times, many ceremonials are scheduled for weekends, so the increasing number of off-reservation workers can return and take part.

Among the Hopi Indians today are many qualified carpenters, painters, masons, mechanics, and other laborers who can secure work in non-Indian communities with no difficulty. The Hopi are shrewd businessmen. Many have proven to be adept machine operators and skilled forest firefighters. Those men who stay at home care for their sandy fields which they dry-farm, or on which they practice flood irrigation, wresting their livelihood from a harsh, though beautiful, environment. Considerable income is derived from the carving of figurines, watercolor painting, basketry, jewelry, and to a decreasing degree from weaving traditional textiles. The average annual income per family is estimated to be $2,050. (Gilliland 1972) The women tend their fertile garden plots;

some fashion beautiful pottery, others weave belts or make baskets. They are famous for *piki*, a tissue-paper-thin breadstuff made of cornmeal and baked on a red-hot rock slab. Several layers are rolled together while still warm. The rolls become crisp when cool; they are tasty and highly nutritious.

All educational facilities for the Hopi have been upgraded in recent years. These include a dormitory housing 320 boarding school students, and six additional elementary classrooms at Keams Canyon, which were constructed in 1956, as was a complete new school at Polacca. A consolidated school at Second Mesa, and facilities at Hotevilla have been occupied over ten years. Formerly, children were educated through the tenth grade; however, the ninth and tenth grades have been abolished and Hopi students go to off-reservation boarding schools and elsewhere for their high school training. Plans have been finalized for a four-year fully accredited Bureau of Indian Affairs high school on the reservation. The Hopi Indians are very much interested in education. Accordingly, attendance is good and dropouts are few. Some 145 Hopi students are enrolled in schools above the high school level. Many Hopi leave the villages after completing school and make their way in society along with non-Indian groups.

Development of paved Highway 264, with hard-topped tributary roads leading to the north and south through Hopiland, has had severe effects upon the Hopi, both in the number of visitors who intrude upon their quiet way of life, and in the number of their younger generation who are drawn away from their hereditary world and culture. On 15 January 1971 a Hopi Culture Center built along traditional pueblo lines by a modern architect was opened by the Hopi Tribe. It contains thirty-three deluxe hotel units, and has a restaurant and conference room. A museum and crafts shops are included in the complex, on Second Mesa.

As one walks by the house blocks or enters the small plazas of the Hopi pueblos, rectangular structures detached from the dwellings add striking features to the architecture. Tall, slender poles, two in number, stand high above the flat-roofed chambers—the kivas.

At Hano, established by Tewa from the Río Grande, clanship affiliations of the kivas are obscure. Every member of the village belongs to one of the two kivas, but when the winter solstice ceremony is observed, part of a clan may go into one kiva and part into the other. Since the Tewa migrated with a patrilineal moiety system to join the matrilineal clanship organization of their hosts, the non-Tewa-speaking Hopi, this may well account for the variances found. When the Tewa were invited to live on First Mesa, they gave heed as an entire community—not by any clan—to their town chief's council. He was chief of the summer moiety.

In the other pueblos of Hopiland the social organization displays its basic Hopi pattern. Walpi, the main village of First Mesa, has five kivas—four separated from the houses, but one attached to a house block. Sitchumovi has two kivas, back to back in a plaza.

On Second Mesa, where three pueblos were built at their present sites in the 1680-1700 period, all of the kivas are detached; Shungopavi has five, Shipaulovi three, and Mishongnovi four. Of the Third Mesa group, old Oraibi has had a long history of rectangular kivas built apart from the houses; but since the total population is now less than 150, the ceremonial organization has suffered decline. Hotevilla, Bacabi, and the outlying farming community of Moencopi have detached kivas in active use.

A respected friend of the Hopi, who spent much time with them and gained knowledge and understanding of their ways, recorded that the nearest thing they had resembling a legislative body was the meeting of the chiefs—"Chiefs' Talk"—held each year at the end of the important *Soyala* ceremony, or winter solstice; other meetings might occur whenever a situation demanded consideration. The chiefs of the ceremonial societies constituted this assembly, with the village chief as headman. According to Hopi organization, the village chief selected his successor from among the sons of his brothers and sisters—the one believed to be best qualified—and trained him for the position. (*See* James 1956:105)

The time-consuming deliberations of the Hopi elders continually frustrated government officials, who wanted quick responses to their proposals and propositions. Eventually, they devised a "tribal council" comprised of a progressive faction and imposed it on the more conservative ones, thus achieving a body with which dealings could be carried on, whether the "old ones" approved or not. When a constitution and by-laws were submitted for ratification by the Hopi, on 24 October 1936, they were adopted by a vote of 651 for and 104 against. In this election only some 30 percent of those entitled to vote cast their ballots. (*Hopi Reservation* leaflet n.d.:5)

This tribal council is made up of members who must be twenty-five years of age, speak their own language, and have lived on the Hopi reservation for two years. Representation is based on village population. After certification by the respective village leaders, the representatives are certified by the outgoing council annually on December first. The council elects a chairman and vice-chairman from among its members; it appoints a secretary and treasurer who may or may not be council members, two interpreters and a sergeant-at-arms who are not members.

From early times, land limits and boundaries have grown to be a problem for the Hopi. After many centuries, the Hopi lands gradually came to be completely surrounded by the Navaho, whose presence became recognizable after A.D. 1500. Some 2,428,000 acres were federally acknowledged in 1882 as the Hopi reservation, but were long in dispute between the two groups of Indians. Attempting to improve the situation, the government ruled in 1937 that the Hopi should have exclusive use of only 631,174 acres and should share the remaining acreage with the Navaho. In 1962, a decision of the Arizona District Court confirmed this ruling and it was upheld by the US Supreme Court a few years later. The remaining acreage (nearly 1,800,000) was held between the two groups "in joint, equal and undivided shares." So the conflict continued.

In April, 1970, the Hopi filed a brief in federal court seeking to drive the Navaho off this shared area and to allow the Hopi living within their reservation, but outside the excluded land, to share grazing rights and leases on trading posts with the Navaho. The Indian Claims Commission meeting in Washington at the end of June, 1970, ruled that the Hopi should have been paid, by the 1937 land rates, for the 1.8 million acres taken from them and that they should have been paid, by 1882 land rates, for an estimated 5 million acres in aboriginal claims. Further hearings and more years of waiting are in store—specific acreages are to be determined and values fixed, or other arrangements made.

SECRET CULTS AND SOCIETIES   A very important feature of social organization among the Pueblo peoples is curing; this is under the control of medicine societies operating within an esoteric cult generally known as katsina. The early Spaniards recorded this as *catzina*, (Hackett 1937, III:131ff.; see Dockstader 1954:148) which would be their rendering of the Keres "K'AH-tseen-ah" or of the Hopi "cot-SEE-nah." In written literature, the word is given diverse spellings such as katzina, katchina, kachina, cachina, katcina, kacina, and audible pronunciations approximating the native language concerned.

Remember that none of the New World peoples had a written language of their own*; so the spellings of Indian words followed systems of the recorders—some simply personal, others in accord with recognized phonetic or orthographic systems. It is likely that this gave rise to certain of the debased usages of today, for readers frequently do not give attention to the fine print or explanatory notes. For instance, Dr. Bunzel in her reports on Zuñi uses *katcina*; she gives a "table of sounds" in which "c" has the value of "sh" and would be heard as "kátshina," with accent on the first syllable. (Bunzel 1932a:471)

Beliefs concerning the katsinas are similar, pueblo to pueblo. These supernatural beings are represented in various ways, all of which are associated in the Indian mind. First, they are *spiritual guises* of an anthropomorphic nature. Again they are masked, painted, and properly *costumed individuals* who appear in the village plazas and kivas as impersonators of the spiritual ones enacting esoteric rites and ceremonies. In another guise, they are *wooden figurines*—small representations of the life-size beings—by means of which Indian children become familiar with the katsinas as part of their religious training and culture history.

When the katsina cult functions fully, every man, woman, and child of a pueblo is supposed to be initiated into it, and every man takes an active, lifelong part in its ceremonies. Men only impersonate the male and female katsinas. Primarily, the katsinas are recognized as benevolent beings who dwell in the mountains, springs, and lakes, and who are the bringers of blessings, particularly rain, crops, and wellbeing. Some katsinas, however, are ogres or demons with disciplinary functions.

Throughout the millennia of man's struggle for existence in the semiarid Southwest, the dominating factor has been rain. Inasmuch as the Pueblo Indians are farmers, their ceremonies are primarily for rain. The building or decorating of a kiva is said to be a prayer for rain or crops. And the feeling is that the correct performance of numerous ritualistic acts brings the desired results. Thus the katsinas, the spirit rainmakers, truly symbolize the climatic drive or weather control of Southwestern man past and present.

Upon death, it is believed, a Pueblo person becomes a katsina; he may appear henceforth as a cloud—that is, as a masked personator. A boy belongs to the kiva of his father, into which he is

---

*Unless some of the Meso-american glyph systems prove to relate to true written tongues.

initiated; girls also may be initiated, but they do not wear masks or belong to the kiva groups. Although the cacique is not a curer, or "medicine man," he has authority over the curers and the kiva chiefs. The duties of the cacique keep him somewhat aloof from the people; on the other hand, the war chief is the most important officer, visibly, but his authority is virtually under the authority of the cacique. Thus, the katsina organization is under the direct control of a cacique and his assistants.

According to legend, in bygone days the katsinas used to come to the people when they were sad and lonely and dance for them. They brought gifts to the people and taught them their arts and industries and how to hunt. After a time the people began to grow their own foodstuffs. When rain was needed the katsinas would come and dance in the fields; then the rains always came.

Pueblo versions vary slightly, but all agree that the people came to take the katsinas for granted. Respect and veneration for their benevolence were lost by some; others had violent fights with the supernatural ones. The katsinas left, refusing to return. However, they taught a few of the faithful young men some of their ceremonies and showed them how to make masks and costumes; as long as the earthly ones followed their instructions properly, as long as "their hearts were right," they were permitted to act as if they were katsinas, and the "real katsinas" would come and possess the persons of the masked dancers. Rain would follow. On this assurance the masked katsina dances are performed to this day.

Serving as a means of uniting man and spirit beings, the katsina masks are very sacred. In some instances they are privately owned, in others they are communal property; they may be kept in certain households along with other ceremonial paraphernalia, or kept in the kivas.

The katsina cult, then, exists for the purpose of impersonating the supernatural rainmakers, so that weather controls may be exercised with resultant moisture for the crops and pastures. The organization is composed of various groups, each managed by a medicine society. Initiations take place in the house of a medicine society. A great deal of accoutrement is necessary. When masked dances are presented the masks may be all alike, or specific combinations, or they may be of mixed character.

Many of the Spanish officials and zealous missionaries did all they could to destroy the aboriginal religious rites. In the Río Grande valley where the Spanish influence became so strong the masked ceremonies were forced underground, or away from foreign eyes, for the most part. Frequent changes among the governmental officials and agents of the Catholic church, with alternating policies and practices, resulted in the Indian's compounded confusion. Within a hundred years after the *entrada* of Coronado and with less than a half-century of colonization, the culture of the Indians had been irretrievably altered. After preceding administrations had rigidly suppressed the Indian religious observances, Governor Bernardo López de Mendizábal, who was exceedingly oppressive in most ways, not only gave permission for the performing of katsina dances, but commanded the Indians to enact them. Accordingly, from about 1660 on, these previously forbidden ceremonies were held in the Tewa and Tiwa pueblos, as well as among the Keres, and even in the plaza of Santa Fe!

Among the western pueblos, where Spanish influence was less disruptive, masked dances continued to be performed much as they were in pre-Spanish times. Later "reformers" in the Southwest found the Indian rites offensive, "horrifying and unclean." But those who understood—some of those white people who were intimate with the Indians and were allowed in the kivas—refuted such charges.

It must be remembered that values differ from one culture to another, and they alter from time to time. Actions that appear innocent to us may be considered extremely vulgar by those of another social group; and things appearing obscene to us may be inoffensive to others.

It is now a rare instance when a white person is allowed to witness a katsina dance at one of the Río Grande pueblos; even Indians of other Pueblo groups are frequently kept from viewing such events. At Zuñi outsiders are permitted to view many of the masked dances. For instance, in the spectacular *Shalako*—a fertility and house-blessing ceremony—masked personators dance before large audiences of white people, as well as Indians, local and otherwise. And in the Hopiland villages restrictions are even less evident. There, some two hundred and fifty or more katsinas are known; the number is highly flexible for a variety of reasons. (*See* Dockstader 1954:23ff.)

Studies that have been permitted in pueblos of the Río Grande region have revealed that Keres ceremonialism is highly complex. In common with most Southwestern Indians, the Keres hold that they emerged from the dark underworld. They have a long myth which recites the facts of their life in the netherland. There they appointed priests, or organized societies, to take their places, and each deity, or group of spirits, taught their human successors how to perform the rituals that were essential to human welfare. Then came the emergence—the coming out of the people at *Shipop* (SHIP-op). It is said that after they emerged they made an extensive trip "around the world"—their world, bounded by certain mountain ranges with specific directional peaks, sacred springs, and related features.

Through the years the Pueblo Indians have been faced with a variety of situations which have altered their traditional beliefs regarding illnesses and curing. Slowly, they became influenced by the white doctors' knowledge of medicine and medical and surgical practices. In some pueblos, or in towns nearby, clinics were established, providing nursing assistance and professional consultations. In fewer instances, hospital facilities were provided. On availing themselves of these newer services, some Indians received sympathetic treatment and kindly attention to their needs; others fared less well, and many were the occasions of long or fruitless waits to secure aid. The Indians reacted accordingly.

In 1950, during the first session of the 83rd Congress, Public Law 568 was passed, transferring health services from the BIA and placing them under the U.S. Department of Health, Education and Welfare. This act was opposed by the Pueblo Indians at that time. They feared that the change would result in less understanding of their problems and requirements. As they came to comprehend the Public Health Service plans better, they became more hopeful. Soon, great improvements in health facilities for the Indians were initiated; and the trend has continued.

Countless surveys relating to Indian health conditions have been made, and many volumes have been written on the subject. Readers interested in learning more on this subject are referred to PHS publications and related sources.

Today, an increasing number of Pueblo Indians seek and receive modern medical and surgical treatment, just as do the majority of the population.

With the Keres, medicine societies as well as clans are important.

Great attention is given to the combatting of disease. The small, secret medicine societies are composed of male members who have the knowledge of the initiated and possess mighty supernatural powers by virtue of that knowledge. Their ideology, paraphernalia, ritual, and ceremonies are grouped together under the term "medicine cult." (White 1935:120) The medicine societies deal only with sickness due to supernatural derivation. Benevolent and malevolent supernaturals being recognized, the latter call forth the services of the curers most frequently.

At Santo Domingo, largest of the eastern Keres pueblos, four major medicine societies are known: the Flint, *Cíkame*, Giant, and *Bóyakya*. These societies work together for the good of the pueblo, uniting their efforts in serious cases. Their power lies not in themselves but is believed to have been secured from supernatural animals. To gain power from these, and make use of it, the curers employ their extensive collections of fetishes and figurines, medicines and numerous efficacious items. Cures may be conducted at any time of the year. The curers wear prescribed attire. Although females may belong to medicine societies they do not know all the secrets. Several channels of attaining membership are recognized, voluntary or by compulsion. In addition to their curative functions, some of the religious societies also have important governmental controls.

The Keres have no moiety houses. Each medicine society has a chamber in which its initiations take place, solstice ceremonies are performed, and retreats held; each society has its headman who exercises some authority over his fellow members. These society chambers, or houses, built in the midst of the pueblo dwellings, are linked with the circular "big kivas" of the Keres system which are used for dances and ceremonies pertaining to the village as a whole. They function intimately in the katsina order, each kiva group being associated with particular clans and with two complementary divisions of anthropomorphic personages. These manlike spirits are recognized as sacred clowns called *Koshari* and *Kurena* (and by comparable terms in other Pueblo languages). The koshari societies do not practice curing; they are concerned with fertility and growth.

The koshari are members of the Flint society which is associated with the turquois kiva—thus the winter people; while the kurena are members of the Cíkame society and function with the squash kiva—the summer people. The kiva heads organize the katsina dances, act as custodians of the masks, and supervise preparations for dances; they also select dancers for special parts such as those who enact the buffalo dance.

Santo Domingo has four other curing societies of minor importance: Ant, Snake, *Kapina*, and *Beraka*. Each has power to cure some ailment. Some of these societies occur in the other Keres pueblos, and similar organizations are found among other peoples.

The legendary belief is that Koshari came from his home in the east, near the sunrise; and Kurena had a home close to Koshari, at a spring somewhat to the south. Long ago, these beings also are said to have lived with the people; but, when they went back to stay in the east, arrangements were made that ordinary men might represent them if properly initiated, costumed, and otherwise prepared. When these personators function it is as if the "real" koshari and kurena were present. Thus they serve as mediators between the people of the earth and their ancient spirits. Those of the koshari organization whom we see are held to be the living embodiments of the spirits of the ancient ones.

Differences in attire and accoutrement, body painting, and hairdress help to distinguish the kurena from the koshari. The trunks, limbs, and faces of the koshari are painted white with black horizontal stripes (or sometimes the bodies are painted grey, sometimes with spots instead of stripes). Black circles surround the eyes and mouth. The hair is daubed with white clay and is done up with cornhusks into "horns" on either side of the head. An old dark rag serves as a breechclout, looped over a thong around the waist and from which cow hooves may be suspended. At times rags are tied about the wrists, knees, and neck. The feet are usually bare. Narrow strips of dried cornhusks are symbolic of the koshari.

Bodies of the kurena are painted in vertical divisions—the right side orange, the left side white. Vertical stripes of orange and black are painted on the face. The hair is worked into a single bunch on top of the head. Ragged loincloth and arm and knee decorations are like those of the koshari. A blue and red necklace made of cornstalk with beads may be worn. Feathers of the desert sparrow serve as symbols of the kurena. But as Pueblo customs break down, traditional features show certain changes.

Members of the medicine societies accompany the masked dancers in rites from which the public is excluded. They also participate in some of the open ceremonies, such as corn dances, where they dance in and out among the formal dancers. Men and boys who dress like the koshari and kurena and act like them, but who are not members of the societies, may dance, too, on such occasions. Frequently, both the koshari and kurena function as clowns to the merriment of Indians and visitors alike. Indian cultural mores provide for a balance of pleasurable or amusing activities and grave or sedate pursuits. The serious duties of these society members, however, are far more important. Each of these societies goes into individual retreats before a dance is held. In

September the kurena society has a dance of its own, and in February the koshari has its dance; obviously these pertain to seasonal transfers.

On occasion, among the Keres peoples, certain other impersonators are seen who are identifiable by knobby protuberances on their masks and accentuated circles around the eyes and mouth—the commonly called "mudheads." These relate to times when the Indians had not yet emerged from the dark underworld. Each Pueblo group recognizing these characters explains their origin as their migration myths are recited. The mudheads serve as messengers of the people and their deities. The western Pueblos place greater emphasis on them. *Gomaiowish*, of Acoma, for instance, equates with Kóyemshi of Zuñi. More will be said of these personages under the discussion of the secret orders at Zuñi.

In the past, each pueblo had a warrior society, membership in which resulted from killing of an enemy and taking his scalp in a prescribed ritual manner. Even though a society may now be defunct, masked warriors' dances or scalp dances may be performed. Patron deities of the war cult are the twin war gods (*Masewi* and *Oyoyewi* of the Keres). The koshari and kurena collaborate with the warriors' society in the scalp dance. Although created as clowns to amuse the people, they have other functions that are serious and far-reaching.

Another important organization is the hunters' society, in which membership is voluntary. It is composed of medicine men who manipulate supernatural power in order to control game, thus assuring plentiful animal food for mankind. Their power is believed to have been derived from the beasts of prey. The society has, or had, its own ceremonial house and considerable equipment. It has a prominent part in the communal rabbit hunts, and plays a role in the buffalo dance.

Among the Tewa peoples, as noted above, the large surface structure of circular form—serving an entire pueblo—has association with the warrior cult. Ceremonial emphases originally were on war, not on rainmaking as is found among other Pueblos. Medicine societies were not part of the social organization, although curing was effected by officers of the warrior cult. The concept of katsinas apparently was lacking in the primary pattern. Later, esoteric organizations with powerful priesthoods, the katsina cult, clowning orders known as *kossa* and *kwirana*, and various ceremonial procedures—largely borrowed from the Keres—were added to Tewa practices.

Among the Tiwa, Isleta gave asylum to a conservative group of Laguna (Mesita) people around 1879, inviting them to establish a colony at the western limit of the pueblo; this is called Oraibi—the same name as that of one of the Hopi pueblos. Two groups of medicine men, who are both curers and weather controllers, function at Isleta—the Town Fathers and the Laguna Fathers. A hunt chief is recognized, and a war chief who is more or less the executive for the town chief and his assisting bow chief.

Properly speaking, no katsina organization into which all of the youth are initiated exists at Isleta, but they have katsina chiefs, the headman being chief of the yellow corn group. Their supernaturals, like the katsinas of other pueblos, are impersonated in dances, but no masks are worn. What katsina organization prevails was introduced from Laguna. The medicine men derive their powers from animal spirits. Clowns, *kápyo*, are associated with the katsinas and appear with their bodies painted in stripes, with spots, and contrasting colors: six represent each kiva and a young boy wearing small deer horns dances at the head of the line of dancers.

It has been stated above (page 23) that Taos and Picurís have chambers used by the warrior cult and scalp societies, and that curing was a function of the warrior society. The clowns are called *Chifunane* (Black Eyes), or commonly pronounced *Chifonetti*; their bodies are painted similarly to the koshari of the Keres groups.

At the Towa pueblo of Jémez, some twenty groups of a ceremonial nature exist, and they include two clown orders, each relating to a kiva; one, the *tabŏsh*, is associated with the squash kiva which has charge of the summer activities, and the other, *tsúnta tabŏsh*, is associated with the turquois kiva which has charge of winter ceremonies. Most of the pueblo men belong to one or the other of these groups; they are self-selective. Women also are members. The tsúnta tabŏsh is concerned with the sprouting of plants, and the tabŏsh with their maturing. The latter group represents the turquois people and the other, the ice people; they are said not to recognize themselves as summer and winter people. The chief of the tabŏsh retreats to the turquois kiva in November, and the tsúnta tabŏsh chief to the squash kiva in the spring. The tabŏsh have two fetishes, or "mothers," and the other order has one. The tabŏsh participate in dances in September and on 12 November, while the tsúnta tabŏsh come out only on 2 August—the feast day of the Pecos people who migrated to Jémez in 1838.

Jémez has no katsina organization, as such, but it has adopted the concept of katsinas from neighboring peoples and has related them to their secret ceremonies, manifest through masked dancers who personate the supernaturals. Jémez katsinas, recognized in pairs of male and female, are envisioned as cloud people, identified with their deceased ones; they bring rain for the growing crops.

A father to the katsinas is appointed by the cacique and is called "chief." He is entrusted with a corn ear fetish, or "mother," and he is in charge of ceremonial whipping. Wherever katsina organizations obtain, the principal initiatory rite is that of whipping by a katsina whipper. Girls as well as boys are whipped—a rite of exorcism to drive off evil spirits.

Ceremonial races of the kick-stick type are held at Jémez on a track oriented north-south.

Two medicine orders function in the pueblo, a fire society and an arrowhead society. (Parsons 1925:49) They treat illness caused by supernaturals of bird, animal, and human form—the so-called "witches." They also engage in weather control. Each group has its chief and each member possesses a fetish, or "mother." The fire society may have women members. The chief of the arrowhead society has charge of the war god figurines. No warrior society now exists. The chief of an under-chief society is in charge of the scalps; this society holds a scalp dance, a function of the warrior's society elsewhere.

As has been noted, the Zuñi have an elaborate ceremonial organization. This includes a large number of esoteric societies, each of which is devoted to the veneration of special supernaturals or groups of supernaturals. Each society has a priesthood, a special meeting place, a body of secret ritual, permanent possession of fetish-derived power, and a calendrical cycle of ceremonies. According to Zuñi philosophy, the sun is the source of life and is duly honored at solstice observances. The most revered and most holy man in Zuñi is the sun priest who has charge of solstice ceremonies and is keeper of the calendar. He is held responsible for the welfare of the community; thus his duties are those of the so-called cacique in Tanoan and Keresan societies. The Zuñi calendar also includes lunar observations.

Utmost attention is given to a cult of rainmakers which is comprised of twelve priesthoods. Membership in these is usually hereditary in the matrilineal family residing in the house in which the fetish of the group is kept. These fetishes are said to be the most sacred objects in Zuñi. Rather than presenting public ceremonies, the rain priesthoods observe retreats in the household of the fetishes; their rites are primarily concerned with weather control—securing rain for the growing corn.

A significant feature of Zuñi ceremonial organization is its emphasis on ancestors, resulting in an ancestor cult. Every Zuñi participates in their veneration, and "they are involved in every ceremony. They guide, protect, and nourish human life," being identified with clouds and rain. It is said that while priests and medicine men pray to special groups of ancestors, the ordinary Zuñi prays to ancestors in general. (Eggan 1950:203)

The katsina, or kóko, cult is pueblowide, including every adult male, but normally not the women. Upon death, a deceased one goes to join the katsinas, but "only those intimately associated with the cult can be sure of joining them after death." Chief concern of the katsina priests is with fertility, rather than with rain.

Zuñi has a strong cult of the beast gods under management of twelve curing societies, in which both men and women may hold membership. This cult centers around the animals of prey "who live in the east, control long life, and are the givers of medicine and magical power." Each society practices general medicine and specializes in certain diseases or afflictions.

The cult of the war gods is in the hands of the bow priesthood, whose members are those who have killed an enemy. It is in charge of an elder and younger bow priest, who represent the twin war gods, sons of the Sun Father. This priesthood serves as the executive arm of the religious hierarchy. In recent years, the warrior society has deteriorated. Membership has come to be limited; some have said the society no longer existed, and others that it did.

In the recent past, certain members, or surviving relatives who possessed the fetishes and other ceremonial gear, have sold these surreptitiously. Collectors paid well to obtain such rare paraphernalia of a passing culture trait. The opportunity to secure like benefits inspired clever artisans (Indian and non-Indian) to produce similar fetishes—fashioned of antler and embellished with feathers, beads, and other symbolic features—and ceremonial pottery, especially old jars covered over with tiny flakes of turquois, and to which fetishes and feathers may be tied with leather thongs. The antiqued specimens show traces of pollen or sacred meal, and readily pass as authentic. About a decade ago some of these spurious items began appearing in the hands of dealers who commonly kept them under cover. It was a while before the quantity available aroused suspicions as to their authenticity.

The Pueblos

At the end of January 1970, press notices made it known that Owaleon, the "last of the old Zuñi war chiefs," had died. His age was estimated to be 106 years. A son is quoted: "Now all the memories of his Indian prayer are disappeared forever ... none of the new war chiefs visited him after he was sick." And the son remarked, "He wanted to be buried at the new cemetery because he believed in God, not in the old way." (Anonymous 1970f) This betokens cultural changes which have occurred among the Southwestern Indian peoples during the past century and particularly the last fifty years. A warrior society continues to be recognized at Zuñi, but the "new war chiefs" have a vastly different role than did the old ones.

The Zuñi run ceremonial races that are contests between the elder and younger war gods; these are of the kick-stick type, comparable to the Keres races. Clan races also may be held, or ceremonial races by kiva groups.

It appears that the social organization of Zuñi is the most complex to be found in the Southwest.

According to their mythology, the twin sons of the Sun Father guided the Zuñi from the undermost world to this world. Here they organized four esoteric fraternities. The people traveled about for many years. Then the rain priest sent forth two of his children, a youth and a maiden, to search out a good place and build their village. The two ascended a mountain where the maiden stayed to rest while her brother looked over the country. When he returned his sister was asleep; she appeared so beautiful that he desired her. His act of passion enraged the girl, and this unnatural union resulted in the birth of ten children, that very night. It is said that thenceforth "they talked a changed language, but there was no change in appearance." The first born was normal in all respects, but the others lacked the seeds of generation, and thus were infertile. As evidence of this abnormality, their seeds are contained within knobs growing on their heads; from the puckered mouth flows unintelligible talk. "Silly were they, yet wise as the gods and high priests."

Realizing that it was not well for him and his sister to be alone, the youth hurried to make things ready for the coming of their people. He created two rivers and a lake with a village in its depths. When the people reached the river—said to be the Little Colorado of today—many were afraid; strange happenings occurred. Following their leaders came the women with little children on their backs. As they became crazed and terrified, many of the children dropped into the water and instantly became aquatic creatures—tortoises, water snakes, frogs, tadpoles, other vertebrates, amphibians, and reptiles. Those transformed ones went from the river to the lake village, the home of the koko, or rain people who have died; there they "were restored to normal condition" and immediately attained maturity.

The rain priest's son who had sired the "nine lastborn children" and his offspring became mudheads, or kóyemshi—old dance men; the mother became the mother of the gods—old dance woman, *kómokatsi*. After creation of the gods, Father Koyemshi decided they must not appear outside of their dance house unmasked. The head of one of the esoteric fraternities, the *Néwekwe*, copied the mask of Father Koyemshi, and others of that fraternity copied the remaining nine masks. The masks are made of cotton cloth of dun color, with a piece of black cloth at the base; under the latter, packets of seeds of the native crops are concealed. A black kilt and brown moccasins are worn; fawnskin pouches hang from the right shoulder. Each koyemshi differs slightly from the others in appearance and conduct. They became the attendants of the koko—sages and interpreters of their ancient dance dramas.

Whereas the Hopi are known far and wide for their katsina dances and their snake dances, Zuñi is famous for its Shalako ceremonial held annually in late November or early December. This is a re-enactment of the creation and migration of the Zuñi people to their "middle place," or *Héptina*, from their sacred lake village. The Shalako—giant-sized messengers of the rain gods—come to bless the houses constructed in their honor (a maximum of eight may be built—one for each of the six Shalako, one for the mudheads, or koyemshi, and one for the Council of the Gods) and to offer prayers that the Zuñi may enjoy fertility, long life, prosperity and happiness. Every member of the pueblo is committed to honoring the Shalako by aiding his clan and kiva relatives; this is done by contributing labor and material goods.

The religious enactments are under control of caciques of the six kivas which represent the cardinal directions, the zenith and nadir. Each kiva has a spectacular group of dancers—the koko, or so-called katsinas—in magnificent attire. The Shalako ceremonial closes the Zuñi year. Their New Year comes near the time of the winter solstice, usually the first part of January. Then the cycle of religious activities begins, and the initial preparations for the Shalako are made; the personators of the dance characters are selected, and households accept responsibility for building new houses or remodeling old ones wherein the Shalako will be entertained. The year-long duties of the personators are assumed; these consist of religious activities, usually held in private, through which the long chants are learned and their presentation practiced.

Date of the Shalako is determined in the fall, and announcement is made that the return of the gods will occur in forty-nine days.

DEATH IN THE WOODS (Keres)

Corn swaying in the rhythm of the wind —
    Graceful ballerinas,
    Emerging at the edge of the forest.
All dip and dance;
    Wind tunnels through long silken hair.
    Golden teeth-seeds.
Trees chatter nervously
    Awakening sky in fright,
    Pointing at Woodman.
A mighty thud! Blow leaves deep scar;
    He strikes again . . .
Corn mourns golden tears,
    Rows, praying for fallen brother.
Jay mocks the greedy beast
    Who has doomed majestic brother,
    His life home.
Wind tosses leaves aside as
    Woodman tramps on his way,
    Ax dripping oak's blood.
The forest, damp and silent,
    Mourning for lost Oak.
    And now remains but a
    Chirp of a lonely cricket and
    Silhouette of Woodman,
    Diminishing,
        beyond the
            saddened hill
                as the far
                    sun sinks.

By Harold Bird, Laguna-Santo Domingo
From: *The Writers' Reader*, Fall, 1966, The Institute of American Indian Arts, Santa Fe, N. M.

On Shalako day, about midafternoon, activities which visitors may witness are begun. The little fire god and his ceremonial father come from the south and cross the Zuñi river; they are followed by a retinue of splendidly adorned personages. After their retirement, intervals occur during which the ceremonies are covert, but the great drama continues throughout the night, with all participants appearing in the pueblo and certain ones dancing in the Shalako houses. As sunrise comes, activities cease and a few hours are spent in resting. Then rites are resumed. Around midday, the Shalako and their assistants come forth for a culminating spectacular which is performed on the south side of the river—the six giant figures, like great birds, engaging in a ceremonial relay race.

One who has observed many Shalako ceremonies has prepared a small publication which should be read by everyone attending this unique and centuries-old enactment. (Gonzales 1969)

The Hopi have been influenced by contacts with the Río Grande Pueblos for centuries and they have borrowed extensively from the Zuñi. They have a strong katsina organization in operation. New katsinas are introduced from time to time, some coming from other pueblos and some from non-Pueblo peoples such as the Havasupai, Apache, and Navaho. The Spaniards brought the horse, cow, sheep, and domesticated fowl to the Southwest, and these came to be represented by katsinas; more recently other representations—even Mickey Mouse—have been portrayed.

We are told that if a first performance by the personator of a new katsina is followed by good weather, rain, and fertile crops, he is adopted and becomes an integral part of regular performances. If such an introduction appears to cause bad weather, drought, and loss of crops, rarely does he come again. The older katsinas are generally held to have superior power, more prestige, and greater dancing skill, but *Hŭmis* (often wrongly called *Niman*)—regarded as originating at Jémez—is held in extreme reverence and is a most popular katsina.

It is said that few katsinas "function as clan ancestors: the names by which some of the ancient kachinas are known are the same as clan names, and living clan members claim that the kachina of the same name as their clan is also their clan 'ancient,' or ancestor (*wöye*). Usually the *wöye* masks are kept in the custody of their respective clan mothers, who see to their safe-keeping, and ritually feed them regularly.

The totemic aspect is present, but very few of the kachinas that are traditionally regarded as the most ancient have any marked totemic character—

most of the apparently totemic kachinas seem of more recent origin, and some are of recognizably alien provenience, either alien-Indian or White. (Dockstader 1954:14)

Only a few of the katsina ceremonies are given on set dates. After the opening of the katsina season in November, with enactment of the emergence from the underworld, any individual katsina or groups of katsinas may be selected for presentation. If the village chief gives permission for a ceremony, word goes out as to date, place, and katsinas to be impersonated. Series of night dances in the kivas are performed freely between the time of Soyala in December and the beginning of *Powamû* in February. The latter is the major ritual of the katsina cult in Hopiland; it is a nine-day ceremony. One of the chief features is the promotion of fertility and germination in the approaching season. Growth of beans is forced in kiva rites by Powamû members, and dramatic performances portray Hopi mythology.

Young people are initiated and learn the many aspects of the katsina mysteries. Then come curing rites, "for Powamû is regarded as having strong medicine for the cure of rheumatism." (Stephen 1936:156) While curing is ostensibly secret among the New Mexico Pueblos, it is under little specific prohibition among the Hopi. Rainmaking receives greater emphasis than does curing. Powamû, or bean dances, are presented and the horned water serpent ceremony, or *Pálulukoñ*, is performed with night dances in the kivas. These two ceremonies are closely connected, the main elements of both being similar. It is early April by the time all of the activities involved are terminated. The weather then permits daylong katsina dances in the village plazas.

After costume preparing and rehearsals, which take place in the kivas, the public ceremony is ready for presentation. On the day announced, "the performers, painted and costumed, proceed to one of several shrines outside the village, where they ritually don their masks. In the regular dance pattern, there may be from thirty to forty performers all costumed alike. These are usually accompanied by six masked *kachinmanas* (kachina maidens), or female kachinas, who are thought of as the sweethearts, or sometimes sisters, of the kachinas. These *manas* are usually men dressed as women. As the sun rises, they start for the village where they are met by the *kachina-amu*, usually an old man not in costume, who has the function of encouraging the dancers, guiding them, and offering to them the prayers of the villagers." (Dockstader 1954:18)

A significant feature of the masked dances at the Hopi villages, as well as at Zuñi (and seemingly in the Río Grande pueblos), is the processional order of the participants. In certain instances the same individual takes a given part each time a ceremony is performed; he is followed by a particular personator, and so on down the line. In the Hopi observances the old, uncostumed man, or "father," usually leads the dancers in single file into the plaza (*kîsonvi*) along a path he has prepared by sprinkling sacred cornmeal on the ground. The meal symbolizes feeding of the dancers; during the dancing the father sprinkles meal on the participants' shoulders and thus feeds them strength. The dancers are led to the south side of the plaza where they line up facing the east. The leader of the dance group is in the center of the line. He shakes his rattle and starts the singing. The other dancers join in, one by one taking up the song and rhythm. Each comes in on cue down to either end, where the poorer singers and novices are placed.

When the songs have been sung once, the father leads the dancers to the east side of the plaza where they face toward the north; the songs are repeated. Next, the line is led to the north, where the participants, facing west, sing the songs again. Then the dancers leave the plaza and go to a secluded part of the mesa, where they remove their masks, smoke, eat, and rest; they also have a short rehearsal of the next set of songs. They return to the village and present another round of singing and dancing. Such a ceremony continues from dawn until sundown. During the midday break, women of the proper clan bring food to the participants. The family of the dance sponsor has the major responsibility for providing this food.

This usual procedure differs from another type of dance performance, which is more akin to the Río Grande pattern. In it, all the dancers are costumed alike; the dancers do not sing, but are accompanied by a chorus of a dozen or more singers—usually older men.

Gifts from the katsina personators or other villagers are commonly brought into the plaza. Then, at the end of the third songset, the dancers distribute them. A bow and arrow for boys and a carved figurine for girls are traditional; now, gifts may include foodstuffs, store goods, and a variety of items.

Other participants in these dances include a number of mudheads, (Coze 1952:18-29) similar to those of Zuñi; in Hopiland they are called *Táchukti*. Individuals may elect to give an impromptu show, or several organized clown groups may take part. They hold privileged positions in the katsina observances and, in their vari-faceted manifestations of jester-great hunter-medicine man, they are immune from taboos.

Still another katsina performance involves individual dancers who may enter a village singly, in pairs, or in small bands. These are the "character actors," some of whom have distinctive actions or calls which give rise to their names; others are known for their unique costuming. They may come almost any time during the katsina season, even while regular katsinas are performing, or in mixed katsina dances.

As the summer solstice approaches, the dance season draws to a close, and the final act of the katsina drama commences. Whereas at Soyala the badger clan ushers in the katsina ceremonies, the katsina clan has charge of the ceremonial departure of the katsinas, when they "go home" to their legendary dwellings. This, the Niman ceremony, usually occurs in July. At this time, impressive dances are given in the villages.

The people of Hano (Tewa) have adopted the katsina cult and considerable of the ritualistic activities from the Hopi, but they have not borrowed the major Hopi ceremonies. They do not have men's societies. Katsina dances, games, races, and other observances—including competitive events like those of the Río Grande Tewa—are frequently held by kiva groups. It seems probable that kiva membership is associated with katsina initiations or with the winter solstice ceremonies. A Tewa clown organization exists; and great emphasis is placed on curing. All religious matters are in the hands of a hierarchy headed by the village chief. A war chief is responsible for guarding the pueblo against enemies and witches, and for settling internal quarrels.

OPEN CEREMONIALS To newcomers in the Southwest, the promise of Indian dances is often a strong lure. The term "dance" as used here has little of the meaning of dances of modern western society, or of esthetic and interpretive dances. The Pueblo Indian (as does his racial kindred) feels he is an important part of nature, that all parts of the universe are interrelated, and that he and the universe must be kept in balance. If this equilibrium is upset by selfish or hostile attitudes, disaster will result. Each considers it his duty to perform ceremonies to help the seasons follow one another in proper succession, to promote fertility of plants and animals, to encourage rain, and to insure hunting success. All this is voiced in his prayers and dramatized in his dances—rhythm of movement and of color summoned to express in utmost beauty the vibrant faith of a people in the deific order of his world and in the way his ancient ones devised for keeping man in harmony with the universe.

Numerous Indian dances are given which visitors are permitted to witness. Some are purely social dances, performed for the pleasure of dancing and having an enjoyable time. To these, non-Indian people and other Indians are welcome. Many of the dances occur on fixed dates, each year (see pages 265-69). Some of these are the culminating performances of rites which have been going on secretly for days in a pueblo—purification rites, retreats, prayers, and sacred enactments.

It is well to keep in mind that centuries of communal life have taught personal restraint. Consequently, the fact that visitors are admitted to certain dances does not mean, necessarily, that their presence is desired. (On occasion, non-Indian neighbors of the Pueblos, commonly operators of trading stores, erect "WELCOME" signs and direct traffic by their places of business, en route to a pueblo that is holding dances.) The Indians may not resent the presence of outsiders, but, remembering that the ceremonies being enacted have been going on for centuries—long before the white man came into this land—we can hardly feel that our being there is a truly welcome addition. We should feel honor bound not to abuse our privilege.

Some pueblos allow the use of cameras—*if these are carried under permit from the governor*, and usually *after payment of a fee*. Other pueblos are deeply opposed to picture taking, and permits for cameras are never granted. Anyone taking a camera or tape recorder into a pueblo should go at once to the governor or his representative and make sure of the existing conditions. Sketching and note taking are also forbidden unless special permission is granted.

Visitors sometimes commit offenses unintentionally, such as getting in the way of dancers, walking across the dance plaza, or standing or sitting in places that cut off the view of the pueblo residents, even to crowding them from their own premises. Others are shamefully rude, making unkind comments about the Indians or the ceremonies they are performing (as if the Indians do not understand English perfectly well), talking loudly, complaining because "nothing is happening," walking into homes where they are not invited, and utterly disregarding the fact that they are attending a ceremony which may be as sacred as any held elsewhere, in church or temple or synagogue. The Golden Rule should be observed in an Indian pueblo as well as—or perhaps even more than—any other place.

Participation in ceremonials is a communal duty and privilege of all the Pueblo people. Individuals are trained to take part in the dances from early childhood. Some of the most colorful and attractive dances are performed by children exclusively, as for example, Christmastime and Eastertime ceremonies at the pueblo of Santo Domingo.

Every item of the dance attire has a special significance—the things worn, body decoration, and accoutrement carried. Spruce or fir twigs held in the hands, or which adorn the body, symbolize longevity and everlasting life. Gourd and tortoise shell rattles imitate the swish of summer rain on the growing crops. Feathers and tufts of down or cotton are cloud and sky symbols. Before he can take part in a dance, each performer has to wash his hair as a rite of purification. Both men and women dance with their hair hanging loosely, the beautiful black tresses often falling below the waist. Crests of varicolored feathers worn on the men's heads are symbolic of the glowing zenith. The women's headdresses—fashioned from thin boards, or tablets (*tablitas*)—are decorated with carved-out or painted figures indicating the sky arch, cloud terraces, sun and moon, and other motifs of a sacred nature. Colors here, as with many aspects of Pueblo and other Indian cultures, have significance such as turquois of the sky, yellow of pollen, green of vegetation, red of life, and black of death, with recognized connotations.

The men wear moccasins ornamented with black and white skunk fur, to repel evil spirits from the feet of the dancers. In the summer ceremonials, the women's feet are traditionally bare, and they are scarcely lifted from the earth—thus representing the closeness of womankind to Mother Earth, and betokening fertility.

Men's kilts and sashes are decorated with sacred symbols in colored embroidery or brocade. Weaving has been a traditional art of the men. The white braided girdles with long flowing tassels represent falling rain, and are often referred to as "rain sashes." The brocaded sashes show a conventionalization of the katsina mask, Broad Face. This design is not embroidered but woven in the weft. These sashes are made by the Hopi men (or, nowadays, by students in the Indian schools or participating in projects which have been initiated in recent times) by whom they are sold or traded to other Indian groups, where they are widely used in dances. Many textile designs have lost their original significance or have been altered in their details, but this particular decoration is always essentially the same in design and colors. The zigzags indicate teeth, and the central diamonds represent eyes. On each side of the eyes are figures called "angular marks." In the black bands, the vertical white lines are called "face marks."

From a man's waist, in the center of the back, a fox skin hangs. This is worn by many dancers, especially, by most of the dancing katsinas. It is considered to be a relic of the earliest days of man, for the katsinas "were transformed while mankind was still tailed and horned." (Bunzel 1932b:870) Often a string of shells is worn over the left shoulder crossing to the right hip; and several necklaces of shells, silver, or coral and turquois beads may adorn a dancer. Above the elbows may be painted rawhide armbands, and at the knees, turtle shell rattles (now commonly replaced with clusters of harness bells) and hanks of colored yarn.

The women usually wear a one-piece dress called a *manta*, secured at the right shoulder leaving the left shoulder bare, or exposing a cotton undergarment of bright color. Silver and turquois pins or buttons serve as decorations on the sides of the mantas. The waist is encircled by a woven belt of red and green or black. Around the neck are numerous necklaces, and on hands and arms many rings and bracelets.

These are the principal costume features of the summertime dances; the same items may be used in varying assemblages in yearround ceremonies. Through them all forms of life are represented: animals, birds, and shells of the sea; vegetation of all kinds; all the elements and features of the universe.

Each pueblo has a fixed date for a ceremonial, or fiesta, in the Río Grande groups, honoring its patron saint as introduced by the Spaniards. In prehispanic times, the Pueblos had certain set or relatively definite dates for ritual observances. The Spanish priests found it advantageous to select the name of an appropriate saint for such ceremonies, hoping gradually to accomplish a transfer from veneration of a sacred personage of the Indians to reverence for a Catholic patron. In part, they were successful. In one way or another, saints' names were applied to specific villages, with accompanying feast day observances.

Through the years, a blending of Indian and Christian ceremony came to be observable. Perhaps Mass is held early in the morning in the Catholic church of a pueblo, with Indians in the

U.W.M. BOOKSTORE

T *	16.95	—
T *	2.45	4221
T *	2.45	
T *	3.50	
* *	1.01	TL TX * *
A * 277	26.36	
A * 277	26.36	MSC TND *
A * 277	0.00	CNG *

000401/08/80

BANKCARD SALES SLIP
CUSTOMER COPY

IMPORTANT: PLEASE RETAIN THIS COPY FOR STATEMENT VERIFICATION

The issuer of the card identified on this item is authorized to pay the amount shown as TOTAL upon proper presentation. I promise to pay such TOTAL (together with any other charges due thereon) subject to and in accordance with the agreement governing the use of such card.

CARDHOLDER SIGN HERE X *Olivia A. Zimmer*

5541079

DATE	AUTHORIZATION NO.	SALES CLERK	DEPT.	IDENTIFICATION	TAKE / SEND
1-6-98		DE 11			

QUAN.	CLASS	DESCRIPTION	PRICE	AMOUNT
		#277		
			SUB-TOTAL	1.01
			SALES TAX	
			TOTAL	26.36

#556

The Pueblos

choir and congregation taking part in the service—with apparently the same reverence and fervor that they bring to their own, aboriginal ceremonials. After Mass, an image of the patron saint may be carried into the plaza and placed under an arbor of boughs (ramada), in front of which the Indians later dance. The Indian cosmography includes many supernatural beings, so the people seem able to acknowledge the Christian God while holding to their own faith. Throughout the dancing Indians may be seen going into the ramada, or improvised shrine, and dropping on their knees before the image of the saint.

Corn Dances   Probably the so-called corn dances, or tablita dances, are seen most frequently. For centuries corn has been the main staple of the Pueblo Indians. It has become more than nutritional, taking on a symbolic character. The corn fetish is most sacred. Corn is exchanged as a sign of friendship. The public performances that we witness occur at the culmination of purification rites which take place in the kiva; these last from one to five days. The corn dances relate to the germination, growth, maturation, and harvesting of the crop and, therefore, are held throughout the summer months. All summer ceremonials are concerned with rain. The corn ceremonies may be very spectacular and onlookers are often deeply moved, even though comprehending only a fraction of their significance.

A typical corn dance, like that at Santo Domingo, may begin with historical pageantry. First, one sees the koshari emerging from the turquois kiva. These ghostly figures encircle both divisions of the pueblo, thus symbolically throwing the protection of the ancestral spirits around all the people. They will perhaps meet the kurena who have come out of the squash kiva, and an excited conference takes place. Runners are sent out in the cardinal directions. They disappear into the kivas or rooms of nearby houses. The spirited parley continues.

After a time the runner from the east returns, and the excited throng crowds round him to receive his message. Animated speeches are made, accompanied by dramatic gestures. The runner from the west comes back, and the same performance is repeated. These are the runners who having been sent to the frontiers, have brought back word about the enemies—Apache, Comanche, Navaho, Ute—prone to make raids upon the Pueblo crops. Then from the north and south, runners arrive with liquids of which all partake—a rite of purification before warriors set forth to meet the enemy. One then sees a dramatization which may be interpreted as preparation for battle. After its conclusion, the participants file back into the kivas, and the historical portion of the ceremony ends.

Where the two-kiva system prevails, a great standard, a long ceremonial wand, will be observed on the roof of each kiva. By watching these, it is possible to know when dancing in the plaza is about to begin. When a wand is brought down, elaborately costumed figures, equal numbers of men and women, alternating, come forth from the kiva. The summer people usually emerge first. They form into two rows and enter the plaza, following a rain priest who carries the great wand. They are accompanied by a drummer beating a large double-headed drum and a male chorus that provide the song and rhythm for the dance.

The wand is highly symbolic. At the top of a pole some fifteen feet in length is a bunch of brilliantly, colored feathers, traditionally those of the macaw. Just below this cluster are bunches of parrot and woodpecker feathers tied on with strands of colored beads and ocean shells. Near the top, a fox skin, bespeaking the long ago, is suspended. An embroidered banner—decorated with clouds, rain, and related symbols—is fastened lengthwise along the pole; it is trimmed at intervals with eagle feathers which float out from the one edge of the banner, and a cluster of small medicine pouches. This wand represents all life in nature. The rain priest stands alongside the dancers and waves the throbbing sacred emblem over them throughout the ceremony. During the course of the day, all of the participants are supposed to pass under the wand as an act of purification.

In a complete presentation of a corn dance, the group from each kiva dances four times, and at the end of the day, the two groups join in a final grand spectacle.

Animal Dances During winter months, the most important ceremonies include hunting or animal dances, variously called buffalo, deer, antelope, or game animals dance. These are dramatizations of the supposed relationship between the Indians and the larger game animals which, during the centuries, furnished their principal wintertime food. Dancers dress to represent bison (buffalo), deer, antelope, elk, and sometimes mountain sheep. They wear headdresses and horns or antlers which make the likeness to the various animals even more realistic. They carry slender sticks in the hands and by leaning forward on these as they dance, increase the likeness.

In a buffalo dance, the leader is dressed as a hunter and several other hunters may participate. The animal dancers are usually in two lines, with a woman, or two, between them. In December, the woman wears a sun symbol on her back and she is called the buffalo mother (or buffalo woman); but in January, she wears a feathered headdress, and is then called the wild turkey. The buffalo mother is the symbolic mother of the larger animal life of the region. At dawn, she goes out to look for game, and leads the animals to the village. The coming in of these animals from hills surrounding a pueblo and the pantomime which follows is one of the most spectacular dramas that one is ever likely to see. Small evergreen trees may be planted in the plaza, suggestive of the forest. Participants in the ceremony enter their kiva after all are gathered in the plaza. They come out and dance four times during the forenoon, and four times in the afternoon. The dancers are accompanied by a drummer and male chorus whose leader wears a Plains Indian costume; for it was to the great plains that the Pueblos had to go for the largest of all the game animals, the bison. The final event of the day is the enactment of a hunt. In the end, the game is "killed," and the limp bodies are carried from the plaza. The other animal dances are performed along these lines.

Eagle Dance The eagle dance as we see it today is a fragment of a ceremony which was formerly common to all the pueblos. It is performed in the early spring and is likely to be repeated throughout the year. The eagle has direct communication with the sky powers and is highly venerated. It is not uncommon, even now, to see a specimen of the Golden or American Eagle kept in captivity in a pueblo, where it is treated with every mark of respect. The eagle dance is a dramatization of the relationship believed to exist between man and the eagle and deific powers. Two young men are costumed as eagles, one a male and the other female; in the course of the dance, they imitate almost every movement of these great birds. One sees them in the act of soaring hovering over the fields, circling, perching on high places, resting on the ground, and going through mating gestures. Although the costume may vary from pueblo to pueblo, the basic features are the same.

 Each dancer's body is painted realistically; he wears a kilt, usually decorated with an undulating serpent design. On the head, is a close fitting headdress covered with feathers; the eyes are indicated, and at the front, is a long, curved beak—in all, a very good representation of an eagle's head; over the shoulders and attached to the arms, are great feathered wings; and a feathered tail is attached to the belt in the back. Being such a spectacular display of artistry, this dance is a favorite with the public and is frequently performed at public exhibitions.

Basket Dance One of the most beautiful and significant of all the seasonal dances of the Pueblos is the basket dance, which takes its name from the use of the food baskets in the ceremony. The baskets in the dance symbolize their normal contents—not only the food which preserves the life of the people, but the seeds that are planted in the ground and which must be fructified in due time; the fruits or grain that the earth yields in response to the efforts of the people; the meal which is produced when the harvest of corn is ground; and finally, the loaves of bread ready for sustenance of the Pueblo groups. The invocations for fertility which occur in a basket dance embrace not only the food plant life, but the human race, which must multiply and transmit the gift of life from generation to generation. A complete series of the scenes presented in this ceremonial would constitute an epitome of woman's life, her consecration to childbearing and the sustaining of the life of the pueblo. All participants are costumed spectacularly—men and women—and the basketry display is outstanding.

Miscellaneous Dances In most of the pueblos, Christmas, New Year, and Easter are definite dance dates. Generally, the Indians dance on these holidays, and on the three following days. A few other dances occur on fixed dates, as will be seen from the calendar on page 265-69, but the dates of most ceremonials are optional and variable with the Indians. Among the dances commonly performed are the snowbird, bow and arrow, feather, butterfly, turtle, horse, crow, basket, hoop, sun, cloud, Comanche, Kiowa, Navaho, dog, pine or evergreen, and war and peace dances. Comanche and Kiowa dances were adopted from the Plains Indians. The idea of frightfulness in connection with the Comanche has been intensified by the enormous feathered headdress—which was never a part of Pueblo costume—as well as by the action of the performance. In the typical war dance, formerly performed in preparation for battle, the body is painted black. Nothing is more significant than this painting of the body: when the Indian painted himself from head to foot, it meant war. This was the supreme symbol of anger and deadly intent. Many of the so-called war dances are in reality peace dances, enacted in religious spirit to celebrate the close of hostilities.

ON CORN (Tiwa)

The green corn stands
in the field
close to Mother Earth
earth worms sacrificing
themselves to hungry birds

Look at their golden
tassels like hair
hanging, touching
earth, close
to moist soil
and getting ripe

I danced for the gods
She danced for me
I prayed for rain
She prayed for me

Singing to the sun
She sang of me

I dreamed not of her
But of animals
She dreamed of me . . . .

By Joseph Concha, Taos

From: *The Writers' Reader*, Fall, 1970. Institute of American Indian Arts, Santa Fe, N. M.

Snake Dance Other than the katsina dances, the best known of the Hopi dances are the snake dances. These are among the most involved of enactments. They take place in late August, in one or more of the villages. Many days of preparation are required before the public dance is presented on the final day: at Hotevilla or Shipaulovi and Shungopavi in even-numbered years, and at Walpi and Mishongnovi in odd-numbered years.

As part of the preparation, men and boys of the snake and antelope fraternities enter their kivas. They emerge, painted and costumed, and spread out on the desert flatlands; equipped with snake whips, they gather snakes over a period of four days from each of the directions. Day after day, rites are performed in and outside of the kivas and other sacred places. Then comes the day of the great spectacle that has long attracted the local citizenry and visitors from all points of the compass.*

As the sun lowers in the afternoon, a single file of antelope priests enters the plaza, singing a solemn chant. After circling the plaza, they line up along one side to await the arrival of the snake priests. The atmosphere is tense and exciting by the time the latter enter the plaza, opposing the antelope priests. In the plaza center is a small bower made of cottonwood branches, the *kisi*, in which the snakes are kept. In front of it is a wooden drum—a heavy plank atop an excavation in the ground. This symbolizes the *sípapu*, or entrance to the underworld. The snake priests stomp on the drum "to notify the gods of the underworld that the ceremony is beginning."

As the two groups of spectacularly attired and painted priests face each other across the plaza, "the gourd dance rattles vibrate to emulate the sound of some giant rattlesnake, and a deep, sonorous chorus that now begins reminds one of some tremendous tempest approaching from the distance. As the song increases in volume, the lines of the priests sway back and forth and, at a climax in the song, break up. Thereupon, the snake men reform in groups of three, and these groups dance with a strange leaping motion entirely different from any of the steps so far used. From an observer, we learn that:

As these dancers pass the *kisi*, the first man of each trio reaches in among the boughs of cottonwood. The priest hidden within hands him a snake which he

---

*At the end of summer 1971, the village chief at Mishongnovi, Second Mesa, made a firm announcement that the Snake Dance there would be closed to the public. Acting without proper authority, the tribal council and the BIA at Keams Canyon attempted to override this statement of policy by issuing their own announcement that public attendance would be permitted. The village chief, upholding his decision, was able to keep the Snake Dance closed to outsiders.

immediately places in his mouth, grasping it with his teeth and lips a few inches back of the reptile's head. The second man puts his arm over the shoulder of the one carrying the snake, and the third man walks behind. If the snake becomes unmanageable, the second priest distracts it by stroking it with his snake whip, or wand.

Each snake priest dances the circle with his snake four times, then he drops it to the ground and the third man of the trio, the gatherer, picks it up. If the supply permits, the first man will reach into the *kisi* for a second, a third, and even a fourth snake. The length of the performance is determined by the number of snakes that have been caught—as many as seventy or eighty—and the number of men participating. . . .

As the dance continues, a priest who preceded the dancers to the plaza continues to sprinkle corn meal on both dancers and snakes. At one point, several women, garbed in old-style Hopi costume, enter the plaza. They bear in front of them baskets containing finely ground corn meal, pinches of which they, too, sprinkle on both snakes and dancers. When all the snakes have been danced with and are being held by either the gatherers or the antelope men, the priest with the corn meal uses what is left of it to draw a circular design upon the ground. All the snakes are then tossed onto the design and the women scatter the rest of their fine meal upon the writhing mass. The Hopi spectators near the spot add their spittle to the sprinkling of corn meal—and woe betide any white visitor who happens to be too close!

There ensue a few minutes of confusion. Snakes dart in all directions, and the gatherers have a difficult time keeping them heaped upon the corn meal design. Occasionally an unusually swift one gets well away into the crowd, and the screams and laughter that follow serve well to direct the gatherer to it. Then the Snake men dash in, seize handfuls of the writhing reptiles, and rush out of the village and down the steep trails. . . .

Back in the village, the Antelope men circle the plaza a few times, stamp on the plank to tell the underworld that the ceremony is at an end, and then march back to the kiva. . . . After the Snake Dance, the entire village relaxes and for four days there are feasting and jollity. Games and races are frequent. . . . Most of the white visitors leave the village as soon as the Snake men have left to liberate the snakes. (James 1956*; *See also* Forrest 1961)

Dramatic buffalo and mountain sheep dances—both very old observances—and a more modern butterfly dance are given in the Hopi villages; these are social in nature to a degree. All three are believed to have derived from the Río Grande Pueblos. Only the buffalo dance is given at a set time (*see* page 266). Many dances are scheduled but a few days prior to their occurrence.

We are told that most of the main Hopi ceremonials are performed twice a year, once as a minor (preparatory) form and then as a major presentation. "Winter in the upper world is summer in the underworld and reciprocal ceremonies are believed to take

---

*Reproduced courtesy of the Caxton Printers, Ltd.

70 The Pueblos

place—a major ceremony in the underworld is parallelled by a minor ceremony in the upper world and vice versa." (James 1956:183*) Ceremonies may last from one to seventeen days, with much of the time spent in preparations.

REGRET (Keres)

I have made a name for myself.
Of this, I am ashamed.
I have failed to sprinkle cornmeal
To the Great One above.
Knowing the day is ending,
I pray to you,
You who have given
The beauty of Mother Earth.
I dare not ask anything more
. . . but forgiveness.
It was evil of me to fail you;
I regret that I have no excuse.
Sincerely, from my heart, I promise,
I will never fail you again.
Whatever the punishment may be
I will take,
But still . . . I am ashamed.

By Rosey García, Santo Domingo

From: *The Writers' Reader,* Fall, 1966. The Institute of American Indian Arts, Santa Fe, N. M.

---

*Reproduced courtesy of the Caxton Printers, Ltd.

CALENDAR OF ANNUAL
.... INDIAN EVENTS

NOTE: Do NOT take pictures, make sketches or recordings, or take notes without obtaining permission. This is VERY IMPORTANT!

In the pueblos are plazas, and the ranchería peoples and other Indian groups have their dance places, where ceremonial events are presented. Many observances occur over a period of several days, but of these the major portions are held in the kivas or in places where only the initiated ones may witness them. Parts that may be seen by the public are customarily attended by adults and children, Indian and non-Indian.

Remember that these are sacred and commemorative rituals. It is expected that visitors will be *quiet and respectful.*

Ceremonies are held in Hopiland throughout the year. The dates of these are determined according to Hopi customs and traditions, without reference to the BIA personnel. Exact dates are made known a few days in advance only, even to the Hopi. During the summertime, one or more ceremonies or dances are held usually each weekend.

Indian dances and ceremonies are based on Indian needs and Indian time. To translate these to the white man's calendar is not always practicable. It is advisable to check locally whenever possible.

JAN 1   Taos turtle dance usually (*See* Dutton 1972a: 3-12); dances in many of the pueblos on New Year's and/or three succeeding days, e.g. cloud dance at San Juan.

JAN 3   Isleta corn, turtle, and various dances

JAN 6   King's Day: installation of secular officers; dances in most of the pueblos during afternoon; buffalo or deer dance at Taos, eagle dance at San Ildefonso. Dancing in the Keres pueblos. Dancers go to the houses of people named *Reyes* (kings), where dwellers are waiting on the roofs. After the dancers perform for a while, the house owner and family members throw gifts to the dancers below and the gathered crowd. Everybody scrambles for presents, but most are aimed directly to the dancers. The gifts include bread, canned and boxed foods, fruit, tobacco, soft drinks, and household items. Many pueblos have dances on the three succeeding days.

72 The Pueblos

JAN 23	San Ildefonso feast day—animal dances in one plaza, Comanche dance in the other
JAN	(Late January) Acoma and Laguna governor's fiesta
FEB 2	San Felipe buffalo dance; also dances in several other pueblos
FEB 4–5	*Llano* dances, *Los Comanches,* at Taos (Spanish-American interpretation of Plains Indian dances)
FEB 15	Dances at San Juan; perhaps turtle dance at Taos, eagle dance at Santo Domingo
FEB	(Usually in February) Hopi *Powamû* (bean dance)—first rites of the katsina cult
FEB	(Late February) Isleta evergreen dance
MAR	(Palm Sunday) Most pueblos, green corn dances, ceremonial foot races
MAR-APR	(Easter Sunday and succeeding two or three days) Dances in most pueblos; ceremonial foot races. Several pueblos observe ditch-opening, or *acequia,* ceremonies with dances; some play ceremonial shinny.
MAR-APR	(During Holy Week, with the climax on Easter) Yaqui Indians have elaborate celebrations at Barrio Libra (south Tucson) and at Guadalupe near Phoenix. Deer dancers, *matachines, pascolas, fariseos,* et al., take part. (*See* Painter and Sayles 1962:24) On the first Friday after Easter, the Tucson Festival Society sponsors an annual pageant that commemorates the founding of Mission San Xavier del Bac. Papago and Yaqui dancers participate.
MAR	Phoenix Plains Indian Club sponsors Scottsdale All-Indian Day
MAR	Gila River Pima *Mul-chu-tha* at Sacaton, Arizona
MAR 27	Dances generally at the Keres pueblos and Jémez
MAR	(Late March) Indian Trade Fair, Pima-Maricopa and Yavapai-Apache communities, near Scottsdale, Arizona
SPRINGTIME	Colorado River tribes hold motor boat races and Northern Yuma County Fair at Parker, Arizona
APR	(Last Saturday) *Nizhoni* dances at Johnson Gymnasium, University of New Mexico, Albuquerque; numerous Indian groups in beautiful costumes (benefit)
APR or MAY	Ute Mountain Ute bear dances
MAY 1	San Felipe feast day, green corn dance (two large groups)
MAY 3	Taos ceremonial races (about 8:00-10:00 a.m.); Cochiti corn dance (Coming of the Rivermen)
MAY 14	Taos San Ysidro fiesta (blessing of fields); candle light procession May 15
MAY	(About 29 May through June 4) Tesuque corn or flag dance (blessing of fields)
MAY	(Late May) Salt River Pima Industrial Fair
MAY	(Last week of May or first week of June) Southern Ute bear dance
JUNE 6	Zuñi rain dance

73 The Pueblos

JUNE 13 Sandía feast day, corn dance; observance of San Antonio's Day dances at Taos (corn dance), San Juan, Santa Clara, San Ildefonso, Cochiti, and Paguate

JUNE 20 Isleta governor's dance

JUNE 24 San Juan feast day, dancing there; observance of San Juan's Day dances at Taos (afternoon), Isleta,* Cochiti, Santa Ana, Laguna; Acoma and Jémez rooster pulls

JUNE 29 San Pedro's Day at Laguna, Acoma, Santa Ana, San Felipe, Santo Domingo, Cochiti, and Isleta—generally rooster pulls

JUNE (Late June, or during July) Hopi *Nimán* ("going home")—last rites of the katsina cult; katsinas are believed to go to their traditional home on San Francisco Peak. One of the ceremonial officers from Shungopavi announced that the Nimán rites and snake dances are closed because "rules against recording, picture taking and hand-drawing have been disregarded again by both Hopis and non-Indians . . . and sacred prayer feathers have been taken away." (Action Line, *Albuquerque Journal*, 15 August 1972)

JULY 1-4 Mescalero Apache *Gáhan* ceremonial at Mescalero, New Mexico

JULY 4 Jicarilla Apache feast (no ceremonies); Nambé celebration at Nambé Falls—special events and dances

JULY 4 Flagstaff Pow-Wow (Check annually)

JULY 14 Cochiti, feast day of San Buenaventura—corn dance

JULY (Mid-July or August) Ute sun dance, Ignacio, Colorado

JULY 24 Acoma rooster pull

JULY 25 Santiago's feast day at Acoma, Laguna, Cochiti, and Taos—dances, rabbit hunt

JULY 26 Feast day of Santa Ana, corn dances; also at Taos

JULY (Late July) Santa Clara festival at Puyé cliff ruins; arts and crafts exhibits, dances (entrance fee entitles one to take photographs)

AUG 2 Jémez, old Pecos bull dance

AUG 4 Santo Domingo feast day, corn dance—large and fine; two groups

AUG 10 San Lorenzo's feast day; corn dances at Picurís, Laguna, and Acomita

AUG 12 Santa Clara feast day; corn dances

AUG 15 Zía feast day of Nuestra Señora de la Ascensión; dances

AUG (Two weeks before Labor Day) Dances in patio of Palace of the Governors in Santa Fe, in conjunction with annual Indian Market sponsored by the Southwestern Association on Indian Affairs

AUG 28 San Agustín fiesta at Isleta

AUG (Late August) Hopi snake dance—a solar observance; in even years at

---

*Since Isleta adopted its constitution, the ceremonial calendar has undergone various changes. One may see dances performed by either the Laguna group which dwells in the pueblo, or by the Isleta group. Dates should be checked annually.

74 The Pueblos

Shipaulovi, Shungopavi, and Hotevila; in odd years at Mishongnovi and Walpi. Usually takes place about 4:00 p.m. Alternately, when snake dances are not held in a village, flute ceremonials are given. The dances are announced sixteen days before they are due to happen.

See note under June (late) or during July.

SEPT 1	Southern Ute fair
SEPT 2	Acoma feast day of San Estéban—corn dance atop mesa
SEPT 4	Isleta feast day, harvest dance
SEPT 8	Encinal (Laguna) harvest and social dances
SEPT 8	San Ildefonso, harvest dance*
SEPT 14-15	Jicarilla Apache celebration at Horse or Stone Lake
SEPT	(Mid-September, or earlier) Navajo Tribal Fair, Window Rock, Arizona—exhibits, horse races, rodeo, dances
SEPT 19	Laguna, feast day of San José; harvest dance and others; trading
SEPT 29	Taos, sundown dance—begins at sunset
SEPT 30	Taos, feast day of San Gerónimo—relay races (early) and pole climbing; dancing
SEPT	(Usually in September) Hopi *Maraüm*, women's social function
FALL	(Some time in fall) Fall Southern Ute Fair; rodeo; Northern Ute sundance
OCT	(1st week) Annual Navajo Fair at Shiprock, New Mexico
OCT 4	Nambé, feast day of San Francisco (Saint Francis); dancing
	At Magdalena, Sonora, Mexico, the Fiesta of Saint Francis of Assisi; hundreds of Papago, Pima, Yaqui, and Mayo Indians (who are affiliated with the Yaqui) converge there each year.
OCT	(Last Saturday and Sunday) Papago rodeo and fair at Sells, Arizona
OCT 31-NOV 2	On one of these days, ceremonies in most of the pueblos; gifts to the padres, and gifts to the dead placed on graves
OCT	(Usually in October) Hopi *Oáqol,* women's social function
NOV 1-2	In the San Xavier cemetery, near Tucson, hundreds of candles are lighted around the graves at night; this is true in all Papago cemeteries
NOV 12	Jémez and Tesuque, feast day of San Diego; dances
NOV	(Usually in November) Hopi *Wüwüchim*—tribal initiation ritual for all boys about 10-12 years

*Because so many San Ildefonso Indians work at Los Alamos, the ceremonies traditionally held at this time of the year have been shifted to the weekend closest to the old dates. The same situation prevails at San Juan, Santa Clara, and Tesuque with regard to dances. Check dates annually.

75   The Pueblos

NOV	Colorado River tribes two-day rodeo at Parker, Arizona
NOV-DEC	(Some time in November or December) The *Shalako* at Zuñi; dancing in new houses and in house of the Koyemshi
	Navaho reservation Nightway and Mountain Topway ceremonies
DEC 3	Ceremony at San Xavier in honor of Saint Francis Xavier
DEC 10-12	Fiesta of Tortuga Indians in honor of Our Lady of Guadalupe, near Las Cruces, New Mexico: processions and dancing
DEC 12	Guadalupe day at Isleta and Santo Domingo—gift throwing
DEC 12	Jémez *matachines;* Tesuque flag, deer, or buffalo dances
DEC 25	Taos deer or *matachines* dance (afternoon)
	Christmas Day and two or three days following, dances at most of the pueblos
DEC 31	*New Year's Eve*, before midnight mass and dancing in church at Laguna, Sandía, San Felipe, Santo Domingo, and other pueblos
DEC	In the various Hopi villages, *Soyala*—winter solstice rites; opening of the katsina season, the purpose of which is to induce the sun to start on the first half of its journey. After this ceremony, other katsinas may appear at any time during the next six months.

POPULATION FIGURES
.... (1 January 1970)

PUEBLO INDIANS (35,351)

TANOAN (10,017)			
Tewa	*3,658*	Keres, western	7,947
Nambé	328	Acoma	2,861
Pojoaque	107	Laguna	5,086
San Ildefonso	358	*ZUÑIAN (5,640)*	
San Juan	1,487	Zuñi	5,640
Santa Clara	1,119	*HOPI (6,019)*	
Tesuque	259		
Tiwa, northern	*1,806*	First Mesa	1,371
Picurís	163	Polacca	755
Taos	1,623	Walpi	81
		Sitchumovi	335
Tiwa, southern	*2,788*	Hano (Tewa)	200
Isleta	2,527		
Sandía	261	Second Mesa	1,435
Guadalupe Indian Village	*	Shipaulovi	202
		Mishongnovi	426
Towa	*1,765*	Shungopavi	742
Jémez	1,765	Sun Light Mission	65
KERESAN (13,675)			
		Third Mesa	1,938
Keres, eastern	*5,728*	New Oraibi	720
Cóchiti	779	Old Oraibi	180
San Felipe	1,632	Bacabi	238
Santa Ana	472	Hotevila	800
Santo Domingo	2,311		
Zía	534	Moencopi	1,019
		Keams Canyon	256
*Unknown			

THE ATHABASCANS (ca. 140,100)

NAVAHO (126,267)		Tuba City Agency	23,043
Chinle Agency	21,150	*APACHE (13,837)*	
Eastern Navaho Agency	28,210	Jicarilla	1,742
Cañoncito	ca. 1,125	Mescalero	ca. 1,740
Checkerboard	ca. 24,785		
Puertocito (Alamo)	920	Western Apache* (Ft. Apache, San Carlos)	ca. 10,355
Ramah	1,380		
Fort Defiance Agency	28,485		
Shiprock Agency	25,379	*Arizona consus figures do *not* include off-reservation Indians.	

78 The Pueblos

THE UTE INDIANS (3,506)

UTE MOUNTAIN UTE

(Towaoc, Colo.)
(est. 1,146 enrolled)

SOUTHERN UTE

(Ignacio, Colo.) (760 enrolled)

NORTHERN UTE

(Ft. Duchesne, Utah) (1,600)

THE SOUTHERN PAIUTE (CA. 1,200)

KAIBAB PAIUTE

(over 100)

SHIVWITS PAIUTE

(150-200 enrolled)

CHEMEHUEVI

(now enrolled with Colo. River tribes) (ca. 600)

RANCHERIA PEOPLES (22,700)

COLORADO RIVER INDIAN TRIBES (4,451)

Chemehuevi, Mohave, Navaho, and Hopi together number 1,120 on reservation and 500 off reservation	1,620
Mohave at Fort Mohave (Parker, Ariz.)	511
Yuma (Quechan)—Ft. Yuma Reservation (1,007, plus 618 off reservation)	1,625
Cocopah (95 enrolled; includes ca. 300 in Mexico)	ca. 695

THE PAI (970)

Havasupai (eastern Pai)	ca. 270
Hualapai, or Walapai (western Pai)	ca. 685
Hualapai at Big Sandy, Ariz.	ca. 15

INDIANS OF THE SALT RIVER AGENCY (3,375)

Pima-Maricopa Community (1,700, plus 300 on nearby reservation)	2,000

Yavapai (Ft. McDowell Reservation)	ca. 300
Mohave-Apache (Ft. McDowell Reservation)	ca. 450
Yavapai Community	625
Yavapai-Apache (Camp Verde, Ariz.)	ca. 200
Tonto-Apache (Camp Verde, Ariz.)	ca. 250
Yavapai at Prescott	ca. 90
"Payson Apache"	85

THE PIMANS (ca. 11,100)

Pima (river people)—Gila River Community; a few Maricopa and Papago included enrolled:	ca. 5,300
Papago (desert people)— main reservation	ca. 5,800
Maricopa—enumerated with Pima	

THE CAHITANS (over 3,000)

Yaqui in Arizona	over 3,000

.... BIBLIOGRAPHY

Agogino, George A., and Michael L. Kunz (1971). "The Paleo Indian: Fact and Theory of Early Migrations to the New World," *The Indian Historian*, vol. 4, no. 1, Spring, pp. 21-26. The American Indian Historical Society. San Francisco.

Anderson, Jack (1969). "Papagos Living in Severe Poverty," Washington Merry-Go-Round, *Albuquerque Journal*, 15 November, pp. 3, 5.

——— (1971). "Paiutes Nation's Most Deprived Tribe," *Albuquerque Journal*, 11 August.

Anonymous (1967). "Archeologists find Apache 'pueblos' near Las Vegas," *The New Mexican*, 23 April. Santa Fe.

——— (1969a). "On Grand Canyon Floor. Havasupai Tribe to Get Houses," *Albuquerque Journal*, 15 June.

——— (1969b). (On Navajo industries). *Arizona Republic*, 12 December. Phoenix.

——— (1969c). "Indians: Squalor Amid Splendor," *Time*, 11 July. Chicago.

——— (1969d). "White Mountain Apache Cattlemen," *New Mexico Stockman*, March, p. 49. Albuquerque.

——— (1970a). "The Peyote Story," *Diné Baa Hane*, vol. 1, no. 11, August, pp. 12-13. Fort Defiance, Ariz.

——— (1970b). "Ute Mountain Utes Ask Industrial Visits," *Albuquerque Journal*, 16 April.

——— (1970c). "U.S. Government Honors Apache Tribes," *Albuquerque Journal*, 26 April: E-8.

——— (1970d). "Indian Tribes Buy Part of Heritage," *The New Mexican*, 1 May. Santa Fe.

——— (1970e). (On Hualapai Indians) *Albuquerque Journal*, 10 July.

——— (1970f). "Zuni War Chief Dies," *The New Mexican*, 30 January. Santa Fe.

——— (1970g). *Albuquerque Journal*, Action Line, 15 February.

——— (1971a). "Arizona's 85 Payson Apaches Stump for Title to Tonto Land," *Albuquerque Journal*, 22 August: A-6 (Washington UPI)

——— (1971b). "Luxury Complex Planned. Southern Ute Tribe Will Enter Tourist Business," *Albuquerque Journal*, 26 November.

_____ (1971c). "Papago Indians Get Farm Grant," *Albuquerque Journal*, 25 December.

_____ (1971d). "Indians Build $2 Million Resort," *The New Mexican*, 16 May. Santa Fe.

_____ (1971e). "Master Potter of Maricopas Crushed to Death under Tree," *Arizona Republic*, 11 August, p. 21. Phoenix.

_____ (1971f). "Ida Redbird Dies," *Newsletter*, The Heard Museum, September-October, Phoenix.

_____ (1971g). "Fannin Asks Indian Aid," *The New Mexican*, 14 February. Santa Fe.

_____ (1972). News Release, Window Rock, Ariz. 18 February.

_____ (1973). *The New Mexican*, 5 August, p. B9. Santa Fe.

Arizona Commission of Indian Affairs (1971). *Tribal Directory.* 71 pp. Phoenix.

Arizona Writers' Project, WPA (1941). "The Apache," *Arizona Highways,* vol. xvii, no. 11, November, pp. 32-35, 42. Phoenix.

Bahti, Tom (1968). *Southwestern Indian Tribes.* KC Publications. Flagstaff.

Baldwin, Gordon C. (1965). *The Warrior Apaches.* Dale Stuart King. Tucson.

Ball, Eve (1970). *In The Days of Victorio.* Univ. of Arizona Press. Tucson.

Barnett, Franklin (1968). *Viola Jimulla: The Indian Chieftess.* Southwest Printers. Yuma, Ariz.

Bartel, Jon (1970). "First Indian High School Starts Classes at Ramah," *The Gallup Independent,* 12 August, p. 2B. Gallup, N. M.

Barton, Robert S. (1953). "The Lincoln Canes of the Pueblo Governors," *Lincoln Herald,* Winter, pp. 24-29.

Basehart, Harry W. (1967). "The Resource Holding Corp. Among the Mescalero Apache," *S. W. Journ. Anthro.*, vol. xxiii, pp. 277-291. Univ. of New Mexico Press. Albuquerque.

_____ (1970). "Mescalero Apache Band Organization and Leadership," *S.W. Journ. Anthro.*, vol. xxvi, no. 1, pp. 87-104. Univ. of New Mexico Press. Albuquerque.

Berry, Norm (1971). "Light in the Desert," *Mountain Bell,* vol. ii, no. 2, Summer. Denver.

Bloom, Lansing B. (1940). "Who Discovered New Mexico?" *New Mexico Historical Review,* vol. xv, no. 2, April, pp. 101-132. Albuquerque.

Bolton, Herbert E. (1950). "Pageant in the Wilderness," *Utah Historical Quarterly*, vol. 18. Salt Lake City.

Brandon, William (1969). "American Indians: the Alien Americans," *The Progressive*, vol. xxxiii, no. 12, pp. 13-17. Madison, Wis.

———(1970a). "The American Indians: the Un-Americans," *The Progressive*, January, pp. 35-39. Madison, Wis.

———(1970b). "American Indians: the Real American Revolution," *The Progressive*, February, pp. 26-30. Madison, Wis.

Brennan, Bill (1966). "This is River Country," part one, The Colorado River Indian Reservation, pp. 9-11, 30-32; part two, Parker, Arizona—the Heart of the River Country, pp. 32-39 in *Arizona Highways*, vol. xlii, no. 2, February. Phoenix.

———(1967). "Parker—Power Boat Racing Capital of the Southwest," *The Parker-Lake Havasu Story*, pp. 16-17. Phoenix.

Breuninger, Evelyn P. (1970). "Debut of Mescalero Maidens," *Apache Scout*, vol. xvi, no. 5, June, pp. 1-5. Mescalero Reservation. Mescalero, N. M.

Brugge, David M. (1969). "A Navajo History," unpublished manuscript. 22 pp.

Bunzel, Ruth L. (1932a). "Introduction to Zuñi Ceremonialism," 47th Ann. Rep., *Bureau of American Ethnology*, pp. 471-544. Govt. Printing Office, Washington, D. C.

———(1932b). Zuñi Katcinas: An Analytical Study," 47th Ann. Rep., *Bureau of American Ethnology*, pp. 843-903. Govt. Printing Office, Washington, D. C.

Carta Contenante le Royanne du Mexique et al Floride (n.d.) Old French map of early 1700s, in New Mexico State Record Center and Archives. Santa Fe.

Chaban, Ruth (1971). "The 1971 Annual Indian Market," *The Quarterly of the Southwestern Association on Indian Affairs, Inc.*, vol. vii, no. 2, Summer. Santa Fe.

Colton, Harold S. (1941). "Prehistoric Trade in the Southwest," *Scientific Monthly*, vol. 52, pp. 309-319. Amer. Assn. for the Advancement of Science. Washington, D. C.

Coues, Elliott (1900). *On the Trail of a Spanish Pioneer:* (the Diary and Itinerary of Francisco Garcés in his Travels Through Sonora, Arizona and California). 2 vols. Francis P. Harper. New York.

Coze, Paul (1952). "Of Clowns and Mudheads," *Arizona Highways*, vol. xxviii, no. 8, August, pp. 18-29. Phoenix.

———(1971). "Living Spirits of Kachinam," *Arizona Highways,* Vol. xlvii, no. 6, June. Phoenix.

Cumming, Kendall (1967). Personal Letter, 21 April.

Davis, Irvine (1959). "Linguistic Clues to Northern Río Grande Prehistory," *El Palacio,* vol. 66, no. 3, June, pp. 73-83. Museum of N. M. Santa Fe.

Dittert, A.E., Jr. (1958). "Preliminary archaeological investigations in the Navajo project area of northwestern New Mexico,"

Papers in Anthro., no. 1, May, 25 pp., Museum of N. M. Press. Santa Fe.

———(1959). "Culture Change in the Cebolleta Mesa Region, Central Western New Mexico," Doctoral dissertation, Univ. of Arizona (unpublished). Tucson.

———(1967). Personal Information.

———(1972). They came from the South," *Arizona Highways,* vol. xlviii, no. 1, January, pp. 34-39. Phoenix.

Dobyns, Henry F. and Robert C. Euler (1960). "A Brief History of the Northeastern Pai," *Plateau,* vol. 32, no. 3, January, pp. 49-56. Museum of No. Ariz. Flagstaff.

———(1971). *The Havasupai People*. Indian Tribal Series. Phoenix.

Dobyns, Henry F., Paul H. Ezell, Alden W. Jones and Greta Ezell (1957). "Thematic Changes in Yuman Warfare: cultural stability and cultural change," *Proceedings,* Amer. Ethnol. Soc., pp. 46-71, annual spring meeting. Amer. Ethnol. Soc. Seattle.

Dockstader, Frederick J. (1954). *The Kachina and the White Man: A Study of the Influences of the White Culture on the Hopi Kachina Cult,* Bulletin no. 35. Cranbrook Institute of Science. Bloomfield Hills, Mich.

Douglas, F. H. (1931). "The Havasupai Indians," *Leaflet No. 33,* Denver Art Museum. 4 pp. Denver, Colo.

Drucker, Philip (1937). "Cultural Element Distributions: V" *Southern Calif. Anthropological Records,* vol. i, no. 1, Univ. of Calif. Press, Berkeley.

Dutton, Bertha P. (1963). *Sun Father's Way: The Kiva Murals of Kuana.* Univ. of N. M. Press. Albuquerque.

———(1966). "Pots Pose Problems," *El Palacio,* vol. 73, no. 1, Spring, pp. 5-15. Museum of N. M. Press. Santa Fe.

———(1972a) "The New Year of the Pueblo Indians of New Mexico," *El Palacio,* vol. 78, no. 1. Museum of N. M. Press.

_____(1972b). *Let's Explore: Indian Villages Past and Present.* Museum of N. M. press. 65 pp. Santa Fe.

Eddy, Frank W. (1965). "The Desert Culture of the Southwestern United States," Lecture at St. Michael's College (College of Santa Fe), 9 February (unpublished). Santa Fe.

_____(1966). "Prehistory in the Navajo Reservoir District, Northwestern New Mexico," *Papers in Anthro.*, no. 15, pt. I. Museum of N. M. Press. Santa Fe.

_____(1974). "Population dislocation in the Navaho reservoir district, New Mexico and Colorado," *Amer. Antiquity*, vol. 39, no. 1:75-84.

Eggan, Fred (1950). *Social Organization of the Western Pueblos.* Univ. of Chicago Press. Chicago.

Eklund, D. E. (1969). "Pendleton Blankets," *Arizona Highways*, vol. xlv, no. 8, August, p. 40. Phoenix.

Ellis, Florence (Hawley) (1964). "Archaeological History of Nambé Pueblo, 14th Century to Present," *American Antiquity*, vol. 30, no. 1, July, pp. 34-42. Soc. for Amer. Archaeology. Salt Lake City.

Emmitt, Robert (1954). *The Last War Trail — The Utes and the Settlement of Colorado.* Univ. of Oklahoma Press. Norman.

Euler, Robert C. (1961). "Aspects of Political Organization Among the Puertocito Navajo," *El Palacio*, vol. 68, no. 2, Summer, pp. 118-120. Museum of N.M. Santa Fe.

_____(1966). "Southern Paiute Ethnohistory," *Anthro. Papers.* no. 78, April. Univ. of Utah Press. Salt Lake City.

_____(1972a). *The Paiute People.* Indian Tribal Series. Phoenix.

_____(1972b). Personal Letter, 7 July.

Ezell, Greta S. and Paul H. Ezell (1970). "Background to Battle: Circumstances Relating to Death on the Gila, 1857," in *Troopers West: Military and Indian Affairs on the American Frontier*, pp. 169-186. Frontier Heritage Press. San Diego.

Faris, Chester E. (n.d.). "Pueblo Governors' Canes," Mimeographed report. 7 pp.

Fontana, B. L. (1967). Personal Letter, 6 January.

Fontana, B. L., Wm. J. Robinson, C. W. Cormack and E. E. Leavitt, Jr. (1962). *Papago Indian Pottery.* Univ. of Wash. Press. Seattle.

Forrest, Earle R. (1961). *The Snake Dance of the Hopi Indians.* Westernlore Press. Los Angeles.

Forrestal, Peter P. (transl.) and Cyprian J. Lynch (historical intro. and notes) (1954). *Benavides' Memorial of 1630.* Academy of Amer. Franciscan Hist. Washington, D. C.

84 The Pueblos

Fort Mohave Tribal Council (California-Arizona-Nevada) (1970). *Letter and Resolution,* 27 October, 6 pp. Needles, Calif.

Fowler, Catherine S. (1971). Personal Letter, 14 June.

Fowler, Don D. and Catherine S. Fowler (Eds.) (1971). "Anthropology of the Numa: John Wesley Powell's manuscripts on the Numic Peoples of Western North America, 1868-1880," *Smithsonian Contributions to Anthro.*, No. 14, Smithsonian Institution. Washington, D. C.

Gabel, Norman E. (1949). *A Comparative Racial Study of the Papago,* Univ. of New Mexico Publications in Anthro., no. 4, Univ. of N. M. Press. Albuquerque.

Galvin, John (Transl. and Ed.) (1967). *A Record of Travels in Arizona and California, 1775-1776, Father Francisco Garcés.* John Howell Books. San Francisco.

Gerald, Rex E. (1958) "Two Wickiups on the San Carlos Indian Reservation, Arizona," *The Kiva,* vol. 23, no. 3, February, pp. 5-11. Ariz. Arch. and Hist. Society. Tucson.

Gilliland, H. M. (1972). Personal Letter and data sheets. *Hopi Indian Agency,* 16 March. Keams Canyon, Ariz.

Gonzales, Clara (1969). *The Shalakos Are Coming.* Museum of N. M. Press. 13 pp. Santa Fe.

Goodwin, Grenville (1942). *The Social Organization of the Western Apache.* Univ. of Chicago Press. Chicago.

Graves, Howard (1970). "Jobs, Tradition, Urbanization Key Navajo Race Factors," *Albuquerque Journal,* 24 August.

Gunnerson, James H. (1960). "An Introduction to Plains Apache Archaeology—the Dismal River Aspect," *B. A. E. Anthro. Paper No. 58.* Washington, D. C.

———(1969a). "Apache Archaeology in Northeastern New Mexico," *American Antiquity,* vol. 34, pp. 23-39. Soc. for Amer. Archaeology. Salt Lake City.

———(1969b). "Archaeological Survey on and near Pecos National Monument—Preliminary Report," mimeographed report, pp. 1-9.

Gunnerson, James H. and Dolores A. (1970). "Evidence of Apaches at Pecos," *El Palacio,* vol. 76, no. 3, pp. 1-6, Museum of N. M. Santa Fe.

———(1971a). "Apachean Culture: A Study in Unity and Diversity," reprinted from *Apachean Culture History and Ethnology, Anthro. Papers, No. 21,* pp. 7-22. Univ. of Ariz, Tucson.

———(1971b). "Apachean Culture History and Ethnology," *Anthro. Papers, No. 21,* 22 pp., Univ. of Ariz. Tucson.

Hackett, Charles Wilson (1937). *Historical Documents Relating to*

New Mexico, Nueva Vizcaya, and Approaches thereto, to 1773. 3 vols. Carnegie Institution. Washington, D. C.

Hanlon, C. J. (O. F. M.) (1972). "Papago Funeral Customs," *The Kiva*, vol. 37, no. 2, Winter, pp. 104-112. Ariz. Arch. and Hist. Society. Tucson.

Harrington, John P. (1940). "Southern Peripheral Athapaskawan Origins, Divisions, and Migrations," *Essays in Historical Anthropology of North America, Smithsonian Misc. Colls.*, vol. 100, pp. 503-532. Smithsonian Institution, Washington, D. C.

Hawley, Florence (1950). "Big Kivas, Little Kivas, and Moiety Houses in Historical Reconstruction," *S. W. Journal of Anthro.*, vol. 6, no. 3, Autumn, pp. 286-300. Univ. of N. M. Press. Albuquerque.

Hawley, Florence and Donovan Senter (1946). "Group-designed Behavior Patterns in Two Acculturating Groups," *S. W. Journal of Anthro.*, vol. 2, no. 2, pp. 133-151. Univ. of N. M. Press. Albuquerque.

Hayes, George (1971). Personal Information. Pojoaque, New Mexico, 18 November.

Hester, James J. (1962). "Early Navajo Migrations and Acculturation in the Southwest," *Papers in Anthro.* no. 6, 131 pp. Museum of N. M. Press. Santa Fe.

Hewett, E. L. and B. P. Dutton (1945). *The Pueblo Indian World.* Univ. of N. M. Press. Albuquerque.

Hill, W. W. (1940). "Some Aspects of Navajo Political Structure," *Plateau*, vol. 13, no. 2. Reprint, 6 pp. Museum of No. Ariz. Flagstaff.

Hodge, Frederick W. (Ed.) (1910). "Handbook of American Indians North of Mexico," *B. A. E. Bull. 30*, part two: p. 186. Smithsonian Institution. Washington, D. C.

Hoebel, E. Adamson (1958). *Man in the Primitive World.* McGraw-Hill Book Co. New York, London and Toronto.

Hoijer, Harry (1938). *Chiricahua and Mescalero Apache Texts.* Univ. of Chicago Press. Chicago.

_____(1956) "The Chronology of the Athapaskan Languages," *International Journal of American Linguistics*, vol. 22, no. 4, October, pp. 219-232. Baltimore.

Hoijer, Harry et al. (1963). "Studies in the Athapaskan Languages," *Publications in Linguistics,* University of California.

Hopi Reservation. (a mimeographed leaflet of information) issued by the Hopi Tribe. 13 pp. Keams Canyon, Ariz.

Houser, Nicholas P. (1972). "The Camp"—An Apache Community of Payson, Arizona," *The Kiva,* vol. 37, no. 2, Winter, pp. 65-71. Ariz. Arch. and Hist. Society. Tucson.

Hume, Bill (1970a). "Sandia Pueblo Adopts Best of Two Cultures," *Albuquerque Journal,* 9 August, p. D-1.

_____(1970b). "Prehistoric Site, Scenic Canyon Boost Santa Clara's Finances," *Albuquerque Journal,* 4 October, p. G-1.

_____(1974). "The Havasupai Prisoners of Grand Canyon," *Indian Affairs,* No. 86 (Newsletter). March-April, pp. 1-2, 7. New York.

Huscher, B. H. and H. A. (1942). "Athapascan Migration via the Intermontane Region," *American Antiquity,* vol. 8, no. 1, pp. 80-88. Soc. for Amer. Archaeology. Menasha, Wis.

_____(1943). "The Hogan Builders of Colorado," *Colorado Archaeological Society.* Gunnison, Colo.

James, Harry C. (1956). *The Hopi Indians.* The Caxton Press. Caldwell, Idaho.

Johnston, Bernice (1970). *Speaking of Indians.* Univ. of Arizona Press. Tucson.

Kaut, Charles R. (1957). "The Western Apache Clan System: Its Origins and Development," *Publications in Anthro.,* no. 9, 85 pp. Univ. of New Mexico. Albuquerque.

Kelly, Dorothea S. (1950). "A Brief History of the Cocopa Indians of the Colorado River Delta," in *For the Dean,* pp. 159-169. Hohokam Museums Association and the Southwestern Monuments Association. Tucson, Arizona and Santa Fe, N. M.

Kelly, Isabel (1964). "Southern Paiute Ethnography," *Anthro. Papers,* No. 69. May. Univ. of Utah Press. Salt Lake City.

Kelly, William H. (1953). *Indians of the Southwest: A Survey of Indian Tribes and Indian Administration in Arizona.* 1st Ann. Rep. Bureau of Ethnic Research, Dept. Anthro., 129 pp. Tucson.

King, William S. (1967). Information from Salt River Indian Agency, Scottsdale, Arizona, 11 April, 3 pp.

Kluckhohn, Clyde and Dorothea Leighton (1962). *The Navajo.* Doubleday & Co., Inc. Garden City, N. Y.

Kluckhohn, Clyde and Leland C. Wyman (1940). "An Introduction to Navaho Chant Practice," *Memoirs,* no. 53, Amer. Anthro. Assn. Menasha, Wis.

Kurath, William and Edward H. Spicer (1947). "A Brief Introduction to Yaqui, a Native Language of Sonora," *Bulletin* (Social Science Bull. no. 15) Univ. of Ariz. Tucson.

Levy, Jerrold E. (1965). "Navajo Suicide," *Human Organization,* vol. 24. no. 4, pp. 308-318. Soc. for Applied Anthro. Ithaca, N. Y.

Levy, Jerrold E., Stephen J. Kunitz, and Michael Everett (1969). "Navajo Criminal Homicide," *S.W. Jrnl. of Anthro.*, vol. 25, no. 2, Summer, pp. 124-149. Univ. of N. M. Albuquerque.

Link, Martin A. (1968). (Introduction to) *Treaty between the United States of America and the Navajo Tribe of Indians*, KC Publications. Flagstaff, Ariz.

Lister, Robert H. (1958). "Archaeological Excavations in the Northern Sierra Madre Occidental, Chihuahua and Sonora, Mexico," *Univ. of Colorado Studies*, Series in Anthropology, no. 7. Boulder.

Lumholtz, Carl (1902). *Unknown Mexico*, 2 vols. Charles Scribner's Sons. New York.

McGregor, John C. (1951). *The Cohonina Culture of Northwestern Arizona*. Univ. of Illinois Press. Urbana, Illinois.

———(1967). *The Cohonina Culture of Mount Floyd, Arizona*. Univ. of Kentucky Press. Lexington, Ky.

McNitt, Frank (1970). "Fort Sumner: a Study in Origins," *New Mexico Historical Review,* April, pp. 101-115. Albuquerque.

Mangel, Charles (1970). "Sometimes We Feel We're Already Dead," *Look*, vol. 34, no. 11, 2 June, pp. 38-43. New York.

Martin, John (1972). Personal Letter. 3 April.

Matthews, Washington (1887). "The Mountain Chant: A Navajo Ceremony," Bureau American Ethnology, pp. 385-467. Washington, D. C.

———(1897). *Navaho Legends.* American Folklore Society. New York.

———(1902) "The Night Chant, a Navaho Ceremony," *Memoirs*, vol. vi, May. American Museum of Nat. Hist. New York.

Miller, Wick R. and C. G. Booth (1972). "The Place of Shoshoni among American Languages," *Introduction to Shoshoni Language Course Materials.* Aug. 9 pp. Owyhee, Nevada.

Montgomery, Ross Gordon, Watson Smith and J. O. Brew (1949). "Franciscan Awatovi, the Excavation and Conjectural Reconstruction of a 17th Century Spanish Mission Establishment at a Hopi Indian Town in Northeastern Arizona," *Papers, Peabody Mus. of Amer. Arch. and Ethnol.,* vol. xxxvi. Harvard Univ., Cambridge.

Montgomery, William (1970a). "Fruitland Mine, Plant Liked," *Albuquerque Journal,* 18 August, pp. A-1 and A-5.

———(1970b). "Black Mesa Coal Provides Indians Jobs," *Albu-*

querque Journal, 19 August, pp. A-1 and A-5.

———(1970c). "Navajo Generating Plant Now Building," *Albuquerque Journal*, 22 August, pp. A-1 and A-5.

———(1970d). "Water Key to Southwest's Growth," *Albuquerque Journal*, 26 August, pp. A-1 and A-5.

Morris, Clyde P. (1972). "Yavapai-Apache Family Organization in a Reservation Context," *Plateau*, vol. 44, no. 3, Winter, pp. 105-110. Museum of No. Ariz. Flagstaff.

Murray, Clyde A. (1969). "Homes in Flood Plain: CAP to Displace Indians," *The Arizona Republic*, 9 November, p. 24-B. Phoenix.

Moon, Sheila (1970). *A Magic Dwells*. Wesleyan Univ. Press. Middletown, Conn.

Nabokov, Peter (1969). "The Peyote Road," *The New York Times Magazine*, Sec. 6, 9 March, pp. 30-31, 129-132, 134.

Navajo Census Office (1970). Window Rock, Arizona.

Navajo Community College (n.d.). *Introducing the Navajo Community College*, 25 pp. brochure.

Navajo Tribal Museum (1968). *Historical Calendar of the Navajo People*. 15 July. Window Rock, Arizona.

New, Lloyd (1968). "Institute of American Indian Arts, Cultural Difference as the Basis for Creative Education," *Native American Arts*, no. 1. U. S. Dept. of the Interior, San Francisco. Washington, D. C.

Opler, Morris E. (1935). "The Concept of Supernatural Power Among the Chiricahua and Mescalero Apaches," *American Anthro.*, vol. 37, pp. 65-70. Menasha, Wis.

———(1938a). Ethnological Notes in *Chiricahua and Mescalero Apache Texts*, by Harry Hoijer. Univ. of Chicago Press. Chicago.

———(1938b). "Myths and Tales of the Jicarilla Apache Indians," *Memoirs* of the Amer. Folklore Society, vol. 31, 393 pp. New York.

———(1941). *An Apache Life-Way; The Economic, Social, and Religious Institutions of the Chiricahua Indians*. Univ. of Chicago Press. Chicago.

———(1942). "Myths and Tales of the Chiricahua Apache Indians," *Memoirs* of the Amer. Folklore Society, vol. xxxvii, 101 pp. New York.

———(1943). "Navaho Shamanistic Practice Among the Jicarilla Apache," *New Mexico Anthropologist*, vols. vi, vii, no. 1. Jan.-Mar., pp. 13-18. Univ. of Chicago Press.

Ortiz, Alfonso (1969). *The Tewa World.* Univ. of Chicago Press. Chicago and London.

Painter, Muriel Thayer and E. B. Sayles (1962). *Faith, Flowers and Fiestas.* Univ. of Arizona Press. Tucson.

Papago Indian Agency (1970). *Facts about the Papago Indian Reservation and the Papago People.* (Mimeographed.) 12 pp. Sells, Ariz.

Parsons, Elsie Clews (1925). *The Pueblo of Jemez.* Phillips Academy. Andover, Mass.

―――(1939). *Pueblo Indian Religion.* 2 vols. Univ. of Chicago Press. Chicago.

Powell, John W. (1891). "Indian Linguistic Families of America North of Mexico." Bureau American Ethnology, *7th Ann. Rep.* Washington, D. C.

Reed, Verner Z. (1896). "The Ute Bear Dance," *American Anthro.,* vol. ix, July, pp. 237-244. Menasha, Wis.

Reichard, Gladys A. (1963). *Navaho Religion,* Bollingen Series 18, Pantheon Books. New York

Richards, David (1970). "America's Silent Minority," *TWA Ambassador,* vol. 3, no. 5, pp. 7-12. St. Paul, Minn.

Robinson, A. E. (Bert) (1954). *The Basket Weavers of Arizona.* Univ. of N.M. Press. Albuquerque.

Sandoval, H. (1971). "Views on 'A Gunfight,'" *The Jicarilla Chieftain,* 1 November. Dulce, New Mexico. (editorial)

Sapir, Edward (1929). "Central and North American Languages," in *The Encyclopaedia Britannica* (14th Ed.), vol. 5, pp. 139-141.

Schaafsma, Polly (1966). *Early Navaho Rock Paintings and Carvings.* Museum of Navaho Ceremonial Art, Inc. Santa Fe.

Schevill, Margaret Erwin (1947). *Beautiful on the Earth.* Hazel Dreis Editions. Santa Fe.

Schoenwetter, James and A. E. Dittert, Jr. (1968). "An Ecological Interpretation of Anasazi Settlement Patterns," in *Anthropological Archaeology in the Americas.* The Anthro. Society of Washington. pp. 41-61. Washington, D. C.

Schroeder, Albert H. (1963). "Navajo and Apache Relationships West of the Rio Grande," *El Palacio,* vol. 70, no. 3, Autumn, pp. 5-20. Museum of New Mexico. Santa Fe.

Schwartz, Douglas W. (1956). "The Havasupai 600 A.D.–1955 A.D.: A Short Culture History," *Plateau,* vol. 28, no. 4, April, pp. 77-84. Museum of No. Ariz. Flagstaff.

———(1959). "Culture Area and Time Depth: the Four Worlds of the Havasupai," *American Anthro.*, vol. 61, no. 6, December, pp. 1060-1069. Menasha, Wis.

Shepardson, Mary (1963). "Navajo Ways in Government (a Study in Political Process)," *Memoir 96,* Amer. Anthro. Assn. vol. 65, no. 3, pt. 2, June. Menasha, Wis.

Smith, Anne (1965). *New Mexico Indians Today.* A report prepared as part of the N. M. State Resources Development Plan. Museum of N. M. June, 279 pp. Santa Fe.

———(1966). *New Mexico Indians:* Economic, educational, and social problems. Museum of N. M., Research Records no. 1. 58 pp. Santa Fe.

———(1968). *Indian Education in New Mexico.* Div. of Govt. Research, Institute for Social Research and Dev. Univ. of N. M., July, 49 pp. Albuquerque.

———(1974). *Ethnography of the Northern Ute.* Museum of N. M. Press. Papers in Anthropology no. 17. 285 pp. Santa Fe.

Smith, Watson (1952). "Kiva Mural Decorations at Awatovi and Kawaika-a, with a Survey of Other Wall Paintings in the Pueblo Southwest," *Papers*, Peabody Mus. of Amer. Arch. and Ethnol., Harvard Univ., vol. xxxvii. Reports of the Awatovi Exped. Report no. 5. Cambridge.

———(1971). "Painted Ceramics of the Western Mound at Awatovi," *Papers,* Peabody Mus. of Amer. Arch. and Ethnol., Harvard Univ., no. 38. Cambridge.

Sonnichsen, C. L. (1958). *The Mescalero Apaches.* Univ. of Oklahoma Press. Norman, Okla.

Southwestern Monuments Monthly Report, Supplement for November (1937). U. S. Dept. of Interior, Natl. Park Service. p. 396. Coolidge, Ariz.

Spencer, Katherine (1947). *Reflection of Social Life in the Navaho Origin Myth.* Univ. of N. M. Press. Albuquerque.

Spencer, Robert (1940). "A Preliminary Sketch of Keresan Grammar," Master's Thesis, Univ. of New Mexico (unpublished).

Spicer, Edward H. (1970). *Cycles of Conquest* (the impact of Spain, Mexico, and the United States on the Indians of the Southwest 1533-1960). Univ. of Ariz. Press. Tucson.

Spicer, Edward H., Phyllis Balastrero, and Ted DeGrazia (1971). "Yaqui Easter Ceremonial," *Arizona Highways,* vol. xlvii, no. 3, March, pp. 2-10, 11, 34, 45-47. Phoenix.

Spier, Leslie (1928). "Havasupai Ethnography," *Anthro. Papers,* Amer. Museum of Natural History, vol. 29, pt. 3:286. New York.

_____(1955). "Mohave Culture Items," *Bulletin 28,* Museum of Northern Arizona, Northern Arizona Society of Science and Art, Inc. Flagstaff.

Spinden, Herbert J.(Transl.)(1933). *Songs of the Tewa.* New York.

Stephen, Alexander M. (E. C. Parsons, Ed.) (1936). *Hopi Journal,* 2 vols., Columbia Univ. Contribs. to Anthro., vol. 23. New York.

Steward, Julian H. (1955). *Theory of Culture Change.* Univ. of Illinois Press. Urbana, Illinois.

Stewart, Kenneth M. (1967). "Chemehuevi Culture Changes." *Plateau,* vol. 40, no. 1, Summer, pp. 14-20. Museum of Northern Arizona. Flagstaff.

Strong, William Duncan (1927). "An Analysis of Southwestern Society," *American Anthropologist,* vol. 29, no. 1, Jan.-Mar. 1927. Menasha, Wis.

Swadish, Morris (1967). "Linguistic Classification in the Southwest," in *Studies in Southwestern Ethnolinguistics,* pp. 281-306. Mouton & Co. The Hague and Paris.

Swanton, John R. (1952) "The Indian Tribes of North America," Bur. of Amer. Ethnology, Smithsonian Inst., *Bull. 145.* Washington, D.C.

Taylor, Morris F. (1970). "Campaigns Against the Jicarilla Apache, 1855," *New Mexico Historical Review,* April, pp. 119-133. Albuquerque.

Thrapp, Dan L. (1967). "Christian Missions Bested: 45% of Navajos Accept Peyote-Oriented Church," *Los Angeles Times,* 17 August.

Trager, George L. (1969). "Navajo Mountain—Navaho Molehill?" *Newsletter,* Amer. Anthro. Assn., p. 2. Menasha, Wis.

Uintah and Ouray Agency (Ute) (1970). Letter, 3 September. Fort Duchesne, Utah.

Underhill, Ruth M. (1938a). "A Papago Calender Record," *Bull., Anthro. Series,* vol. 2, no. 5, 1 March, 64 pp. Albuquerque.

_____(1938b). *Singing for Power.* Univ. of Calif. Press. Berkeley.

_____(1940). *The Papago Indians of Arizona,* Sherman Pamphlets, no. 3, 63 pp. Education Division, U. S. Office of Indian Affairs.

Ute Mountain Ute Agency, Towaoc, Colorado (n.d.[a], 1969?). "The American Indians of Colorado," 5 pp. Mimeographed report.

_____(n.d.[b], 1969?). "A Brief History of the Colorado Utes," 3 pp. Mimeographed report.

_____(1970). Letter, 18 August.

Van Valkenburgh, Richard (1945). "The Government of the Navajos," *Ariz. Quarterly,* vol. 1, pp. 63-73. Univ. of Ariz. Press. Tucson.

Vestal, Paul A. (1952). "Ethnobotany of the Rimrock Navaho," *Papers.* Peabody Mus. of Amer. Arch. and Ethnol., vol. 40, no. 4. Harvard Univ. Cambridge.

Vogt, Evon Z. (1951). "Navaho Veterans—a Study of Changing Values," *Papers,* Peabody Mus. of Amer. Arch. and Ethnol., vol. xli, no. 1. Harvard Univ. Cambridge.

Waliczed, John (1970). "Navajo High School Opens Door at Home," *The New Mexican,* 6 September (from Gallup Independent for AP). Santa Fe.

Walker, George W. (1970). "Celebrating the Arrival of Dr. Charles H. Cook, after Whom Cook Training School is Named, at Sacaton, Arizona," *Indian Highways,* no. 134, December, pp. 4 and 6. Cook Christian Training School. Tempe, Ariz.

White, Leslie A. (1935). "The Pueblo of Santo Domingo, New Mexico," *Memoirs* of the Amer. Anthro. Assn., no. 43, pp. 1-210. Menasha, Wis.

Whitfield, Charles (1971). Personal Information, long distance phone call, 11 May.

Whiting, Alfred F. (1958). "Havasupai Characteristics in the Cohonina," *Plateau,* vol. 30, no. 30, January, pp. 55-60. Museum of No. Ariz. Flagstaff.

Whitman, William III (1947). "The Pueblo Indians of San Ildefonso," *Contribs. to Anthropology, Columbia Univ.* no. 34. New York.

Willey, Gordon R. (1966). *An Introduction to American Archaeology,* vol. I. Prentice-Hall, Inc. Englewood Cliffs, New Jersey.

Yazzie, Ethelou (Ed.) (1971). *Navajo History,* vol. I. Navajo Community College Press. Many Farms, Arizona.

Young, Robert W. (1961) "The Origin and Development of Navajo Tribal Government," *The Navajo Yearbook,* Report no. viii, 1951-1961 a Decade of Progress, pp. 371-392. Navajo Agency. Window Rock, Ariz.

_____(1968). *The Role of the Navajo in the Southwestern Drama.* Robert W. Young and *The Gallup Independent.* Galley, N.M.

Young, Robert W., and William Morgan (1943). *The Navaho Language.* Education Div., U. S. Indian Service Phoenix.